Basketball's Greatest Stars

by Al Hirshberg

G. P. Putnam's Sons   New York

Recent books in PUTNAM'S SPORTS SHELF

Third Impression

© 1963 by Al Hirshberg

All rights reserved
Published simultaneously in the Dominion of
Canada by Longmans Canada Limited, Toronto

Library of Congress Catalog Card Number: 63-7741

MANUFACTURED IN THE UNITED STATES OF AMERICA

10-up

CONTENTS

FOREWORD

While the men whose stories are told in this book are or were players or coaches of prominence, this was not Al Hirshberg's only consideration in selecting them as his subjects. He picked them as personalities as well as athletes, and, in writing of them as personalities, he told their stories in his own way. Since it is as a writer of personality pieces that Al is at his best, he has made this one of the finest basketball books I have ever read.

Although there are occasional exceptions, most athletes are very nice people indeed. Their family ties are close, their sense of responsibility strong, their pride great, their instincts decent.

This is particularly true of those basketball players on whom I think I qualify as an authority. I have played with them, worked with them and coached them almost all my life, and I know them as well as anyone does. They are nearly all college men; they know what is expected of them off the court as well as on it, and they act accordingly. In this book, Al Hirshberg has probed into the human, as well as the basketball, side of their natures.

I can understand this well, for I believe much of my success as coach of the Boston Celtics stems from my knowledge of human nature and my application of this knowledge to my own athletes. Hirshberg knows human nature, too, as I learned when I worked with him on a major magazine article about my team, which I am convinced is the greatest ever assembled in the history of basketball.

All of the personalities covered in this book are champions in their own way. Some may never have actually won titles, but their failures have not been their own. They are all people of class and stature, as well as tremendous basketball ability. There is no player I would not be delighted to have on my own ball club. The coach who couldn't win with these fellows is in the wrong business.

Anyone who reads this book will come away with new knowledge of what makes great players and coaches click. Al Hirshberg has caught them all in sharp relief. He has picked the cream of the crop. I can't recommend this book too highly. It is entertaining, informative and authoritative, and I'm proud to be included as one of the subjects.

Arnold (Red) Auerbach
Coach of the world's champion Boston Celtics

1

GEORGE MIKAN

Probably no athlete in history ever dominated a game as thoroughly as George Mikan dominated professional basketball from 1947 to 1954. Mikan was more than a basketball star. He represented an era. When he was in his prime, he rewrote the record books, and the Minneapolis Lakers, for whom he starred, were champions of all they surveyed.

Mikan was the Lakers. This giant of a man, six feet, ten inches tall and weighing 245 pounds, was so near-sighted that he wore glasses a quarter of an inch thick, yet he was the outstanding star of his time and he made the Lakers the outstanding team. With him, they were kings of the basketball universe; without him, they were nothing. When Mikan retired permanently after a brief comeback in 1956, the Lakers folded, not just a little, but completely. Four years later, their franchise, once the richest in the game, had deteriorated so badly that it was moved to Los Angeles, leaving Minneapolis only memories of a golden basketball age.

But what memories!

Starting with the 1947–48 season, when the Lakers won the championship of the old National Basketball League, they were the cream of the pro game's crop. After they joined what is now the National Basketball Association in 1948, they won five titles in six years, thanks to Mikan. There were other men on this great team, but everyone in basketball, including themselves, realized they made up only the supporting cast for an amazing star.

Mikan was the league's top scorer, its best rebounder, its roughest customer and one of its cagiest operators. Partly because of him, at least two basketball rules were changed. At his best in the clutches, he won the games that had to be won and scored the baskets that had to be scored.

In nine seasons as a professional, Mikan piled up 11,764 points and had a lifetime average of 22.6 points per game. He led the league in scoring in the three years between 1949 and 1951, during which period he averaged more than than 28 points a game, which was fantastic for the time. In those days, 100-point games were rare. It was only in later years that they became so commonplace that even losing teams often had 100 or more points. The records that Mikan left have been broken only because the game has changed, not necessarily because the athletes have improved.

When Mikan was in his heyday, there was no 24-second rule, requiring that the team in possession of the ball must take a shot at the basket within that period. Teams could hold the ball as long as they were able to keep it away from the opposition. The Lakers took their time getting the ball into scoring position, then fed it to Mikan when he arrived at the keyhole.

Mikan was sometimes a long time getting there, for his major weakness was lack of speed. The Lakers' slogan, "Wait for Mikan," became a catch phrase all over the league. He was worth waiting for. Once he arrived, it was almost a sure basket. Because of his height and strength, he was nearly impossible to stop under the hoop.

There is an endless argument in basketball circles over what Mikan could achieve in N.B.A. competition today. A professional star who played against Mikan, and not one of his admirers, once remarked, "He wouldn't be worth a nickel with the 24-second rule. Why, it took him pretty nearly that long to get from one end of the court to the other."

Other detractors have pointed out that while Mikan was the only graceful big man in the league, every team has graceful big men today. While this is true enough, it doesn't mean that Mikan would be lost in the shuffle. There's no question in the minds of many experts that he could hold his own against titans like Wilt Chamberlain, Bill Russell and Bob Pettit, all great athletes as well as unusually big men.

For Mikan was a great athlete, too. He was a good enough baseball pitcher to attract major league bids, which he turned down in favor of basketball. While not fast on his feet, he was quick in his movements and he had marvelous reflexes. Aside from all this, he was a deadly shooter, a cool performer when the chips were down and one of the most rugged men ever to play pro basketball.

The cry around the league wasn't "Break up the Lakers," but "Break up Mikan." George was tough because he had to be in order to survive. Everyone in the league was gunning for him. Throughout his N.B.A. career, he never had an easy game. Every team double-teamed and triple-teamed him, and he was constantly pushing opponents away, like an elephant shaking off flies. Big as he was, he took an unbelievable beating. After each game, his huge body was a mass of bruises.

In self-defense, Mikan became a master at throwing his weight around. His hips, elbows and shoulders became protective weapons, with the result that he drew more personal fouls than big men draw today. Yet he was so clever that he rarely fouled out of a game. He often started the final quarter with five personals charged against him, yet avoided the sixth that would have sent him to the sidelines. This meant absorbing a terrible beating, but he accepted it as part of his job.

Once, after a particularly rough game, during which Mikan took far more than he dished out, he was told in the locker room that opposing players claimed he had got away with murder all night.

"*I* got away with murder?" he repeated, angrily indicating the welts on his arms and legs and torso. "What do you think these are—cherry blossoms?"

Mikan made the All-Star team every year in which he played, and he spread-eagled the league so completely that there was serious talk of legislating against him. The N.B.A. finally doubled the size of the foul shooting lane, from six feet to twelve, a move that was aimed directly at big men in general and Mikan in particular. The rule made it more difficult for any one man to dominate the play under the basket when rebounds came off the boards on missed foul shots.

Even before he turned professional, Mikan was the primary cause of another rule change aimed at tall men. While at De Paul University in Chicago, George became one of the best "goal-tenders" in college basketball. This maneuver can be performed successfully only by a big man, for it entails jumping high enough to reach above the basket and bat the ball out before it drops through the hoop. It was legal when Mikan entered college, but ruled out before he graduated.

Most athletes show some aptitude for sports as youngsters, but not George Mikan. He was abnormally large as a kid growing up in Joliet, Illinois, and terribly sensitive about his height. As long as he could remember, he towered over his classmates, who teased him unmercifully. Despite the fact that he had two younger brothers, he crawled into a shell and stayed there for years.

George's parents, both of whom were of average height, ran a restaurant and bar and although they were never rich, they never starved either. While he was in grammar school, George's grandmother bought a piano, which fascinated him. His earliest ambition was to become a concert artist. Unlike other kids who spend their lives figuring out ways of avoiding piano lessons, George enjoyed them. He might have taken music seriously except for the barbs that came his way from other children his age. He couldn't take any more taunts, so he gave up the lessons.

His first real triumph came at the age of ten, when he won the marble-shooting championship of Will County. This earned him a day as honorary mayor of Joliet and a trip to Chicago to have his picture taken with Babe Ruth. For many years that was the proudest moment of his life, and he still remembers it with nostalgia.

The status that he won with his marble championship didn't last long. Soon the other kids were making life miserable for Mikan, and by the time he was in high school, he was going around with a chip on his shoulder. Once, in exasperation, he knocked down another boy and when the youth hit his head on the sidewalk, George was afraid he had killed him. The youngster's injury wasn't serious, however, but George never forgot the unmerciful tongue-lashing he got from the principal.

He showed little interest in sports until just before.he started at Joliet High School. Then, as the tallest boy of his age in town, he was a natural for Joliet's Catholic Youth Organization basketball team. Both George and his brother, Ed, who later followed him into De Paul and pro basketball, played for the C.Y.O., and if life had proceeded along normal lines for George, he would probably have played for the high school team as well.

But a C.Y.O. basketball injury stopped his high school career before it got started. In a game against the Waukegan C.Y.O. team, George brought his foot down hard on the bounding ball and suffered a leg break so complicated that he couldn't walk properly for a year and a half. When the family doctor realized how serious it was, he told George that he'd never again be able to play basketball.

The leg fracture was the first of an awesome series of injuries which Mikan suffered. Basketball is not considered a dangerous sport, and it isn't for most people. But Mikan was one of the most brittle men who ever played. He was so injury-prone that after a while he ignored all but the most crippling mishaps. Once he went through two playoff games with a broken wrist. He played scores of times with broken fingers, and a broken nose failed to keep him on the sidelines.

His list of injuries during his college and professional career sounds like the log of a hospital emergency ward. Among other things, he had another leg break, an ankle break, two wrist fractures, a broken nose, innumerable finger breaks, the loss of several teeth and a collection of cuts, slashes and punctures that required a total of 166 stitches.

But nothing had as sobering an effect on him as his first broken leg, for while he was convalescing he decided he wanted to become a priest. The Mikans had always been devout Catholics, and George's mother was delighted when he told her.

When he was able to return to school, George entered Quigley Preparatory Seminary in Chicago, and from then on he was too busy for basketball. It took him three hours a day just to commute to school from his home, and his study load was tremendous. In the meantime, he kept growing like a weed, and by the time he graduated at the age of seventeen, he stood six feet, eight and a half inches and weighed 240 pounds.

By this time, he had changed his mind about the priesthood and wanted to enter Notre Dame. He went to South Bend in hopes of getting a basketball scholarship, but George Keogan, the Notre Dame coach, after watching him for a few moments, told him to forget it.

"You'll never be a basketball player," Keogan said. "You're too clumsy."

As the discouraged youth started to leave the gymnasium, he was approached by Keogan's assistant, a young coach named Ray Meyer.

"Don't let it get you down, kid," Meyer said. "Stick with it, and some day you'll be a fine player."

Three weeks later, Mikan, still shopping around for a

college he could afford, walked into the De Paul University gym. The first person he saw there was Ray Meyer, who had just become the varsity basketball coach. It was a happy, history-making coincidence for everybody concerned. Meyer made a star out of Mikan and Mikan put De Paul on the basketball map.

Besides making All-American teams three years in a row, George led De Paul to one National Invitation Tournament championship and prominence in both N.I.T. and N.C.A.A. tournaments in the years between 1943 and 1946. He also pitched for the baseball team, attracting the attention of several scouts in the Chicago area.

But while he liked baseball, basketball was his game, and he knew it. By the time he graduated in 1946, Mikan was the nation's outstanding college basketball star, and was swamped with professional offers. He took the one that sounded the most attractive, a five-year, $60,000 contract with the Chicago Gears in the National Basketball League.

The Gears folded after one season, but what first appeared to be a bad break was quickly transformed when Mikan's contract was picked up by the Lakers. Just as in the case of Meyer and De Paul, this turned out to be an alliance that benefited everyone. The Lakers, coached by young Johnny Kundla, needed a big man to turn a good team into a great one, and Mikan was exactly the one they were looking for.

The shift meant more than just a change of uniforms to Mikan. He and Patricia Lu Deveny had been married only a few months, and both wanted to settle down away from the Chicago area. They moved to Minneapolis, and liked it so much that they live there to this day.

In 1947, the future of professional basketball was shaky.

The N.B.L. was dying and the new Basketball Association of America (later the National Basketball Association) was fighting for recognition. The Lakers were in the N.B.L., but the league was full of weak franchises. A year after Mikan helped the Lakers win the N.B.L. title, the two leagues merged, and that marked the real beginning of what is still known as the era of George Mikan.

The pro game had been starving for a hot drawing card, and Mikan was it. He drew customers wherever he went, and he packed them in at home. Minneapolis and St. Paul sports fans who previously wouldn't have walked across the street to see a basketball game flocked to the Minneapolis Auditorium to see Mikan in action. Better still, the same thing happened in other towns when the Lakers were the visiting team.

"Mikan helped the whole league," a former official of the N.B.A. declared. "And it's no exaggeration to say he saved it. We weren't much better off than the N.B.L. until he came along."

Mikan's first-year statistics were nothing less than awesome. He set practically every record in the league in everything except total points for a single game, 63, made by Joe Fulks of Philadelphia. But Mikan's name appeared twenty-five times for scoring 30 or more points in a single game, and he led the league in goals, fouls and total points. It was the same story the next year, and the year after that. He didn't lead the league in scoring after 1951, but he was always close to the top, always high on the list of scorers in individual games and always on the All-Star team.

Mikan's real value to the Lakers rarely showed in the statistics. When they needed a key basket late in a playoff game, it was Mikan who scored it. When the result of a title game was riding in the balance, it was Mikan who settled the issue. He was the big man, in action as well as size, in the winning of all five titles the Lakers won between 1948 and 1954.

"He's six feet, ten inches, and he couldn't be greater if he were ten feet, six inches," wrote Oscar Fraley of the United Press.

Fraley was quite right. Mikan's value to the Lakers was proved beyond doubt in 1951, the one season in which they failed to win the playoffs. Mikan broke his ankle early in the semifinals against the Rochester Royals. It was one injury he couldn't ignore. Without him, the Lakers fell apart, and the Royals went on to win the championship.

Mikan's retirement came unexpectedly, for he still seemed to be in his prime when he hung up his sneakers. On September 25, 1954, he walked into the Lakers' office in Minneapolis and announced he was through. He had passed the bar two years before and his law practice was taking up more and more of his time. He had front office duties to perform for the Lakers. But perhaps most important, he was sick of the incessant pounding he had to take every time he went out to the basketball floor.

He served for a while as the Lakers' general manager and did a brief hitch as coach of the club, but the team couldn't get along with him out of uniform. His comeback in 1956 lasted for 37 games, during which he scored 390 points, then he quit for good.

The end of Mikan meant the end of professional basketball for Minneapolis. The game there never recovered from the blow of George's final retirement. He left a void which no man, no matter how great or how colorful, could fill.

Today George Mikan is a highly successful Minneapolis

attorney, but his home is full of basketball mementos and his head is full of memories. Perhaps the most vivid is of the time he was chosen basketball's man of the half century by *Sport Magazine*. He had every reason to be proud of the company in which he found himself.

"What Babe Ruth was to baseball," an observer wrote at the time, "what Bobby Jones was to golf, what Bill Tilden was to tennis, what Jack Dempsey was to boxing, George Mikan was to basketball."

It was a fitting tribute to a great athlete. Even his worst enemy couldn't deny that Mikan richly deserved it.

Hank Luisetti

2

HANK LUISETTI

Until Angelo Enrico (Hank) Luisetti flashed like a meteor across the nation's sports horizon in the midthirties, basketball never had a hero. It hasn't had one quite like him since, and probably never will. Luisetti, besides being the most popular basketball player of all time, left an indelible imprint on the game. With the help of a spectacularly accurate one-handed shot which defied all custom in an age which preached two hands for everybody, Luisetti snatched basketball away from the purists and gave it to the public. All by himself, he started the transformation of a somewhat stuffy game into the wide open sport it is today.

It took more than basketball ability to make Luisetti the idol he became, but he had all the necessary ingredients. Six feet, three and a half inches tall, dark-haired, graceful, beautifully built, this handsome, fun-loving product of the San Francisco waterfront was an Adonis with the soul of a pixie. He loved basketball so much that he grinned while he played it. He was smooth, effortless and amazingly versatile, for he could run, dribble and pass, as well as shoot. Marked for special fame almost from the moment he entered Stanford as a freshman in 1934, Luisetti not only revolutionized basketball, but he became a national figure as much in the mold of Frank Sinatra as of Babe Ruth.

Long before he graduated from college, Luisetti attracted crowds wherever he went. Men admired him and girls manhandled him. He got letters from all over the world, phone calls from all over the country. He needed a police escort to get from the arena to his hotel in Cleveland one night. His clothes were almost ripped off his back after he starred in a game at Denver. In Los Angeles, hysterical females of all ages clawed each other to get near him. He wasn't safe even on his own campus at Palo Alto. There were times when he had to walk across it wearing a catcher's mask for protection against the attentions of ardent co-eds.

He got $10,000 for making a movie with Betty Grable, but turned down several times that amount in professional offers. When the A.A.U. deprived him of his amateur standing anyhow, such a tremendous wave of resentment swept the country that the order was revoked.

Luisetti, a local legend by his junior year, leaped to national prominence in one unforgettable night in December of 1936 at New York's Madison Square Garden. Even as it is today, this was the mecca of college basketball—and a classic stumbling block for upstart teams from the West, which had never had good luck there. Stanford was considered an upstart team by the sophisticated Eastern experts. They had heard all about the Indians and their one-handed miracle man. Not a single one gave Stanford a chance against mighty Long Island University, which was riding on the wings of a 43-game winning streak.

"Nobody can tell me shooting with one hand is sound basketball," rumbled Nat Holman, the C.C.N.Y. coach. "They'll never get me to teach it to my boys."

Luisetti made him eat the words. While a capacity crowd of 18,000 watched in amazement, the Stanford star put on a remarkable show. He was all over the court, passing and running, grinning with the sheer joy of playing the game he loved, and shooting baskets with both left hand and right, but never the two together.

Madison Square Garden fans went wild for him. When he came off the court after pacing the Indians to an astounding 45–31 upset victory with 15 points of his own, they gave him a standing ovation.

Hank Luisetti was made—and so was the one-handed shot, which has since become an integral part of every good basketball player's equipment.

Stanford ripped through the rest of its Eastern tour undefeated, the first Western basketball team ever to score a sweep on the Atlantic seaboard. The Indians went on to win the national championship with 25 victories and only 2 defeats, as well as their second straight of three Pacific Coast Conference titles. A year later they returned to the Garden and whipped L.I.U. and C.C.N.Y. on successive nights, thanks to Luisetti's remarkable one-handed shots. By that time even Nat Holman was convinced.

By today's standards, Luisetti's scoring records were nothing to write home about, but by the standards of his time they were fantastic. He scored 1596 points during his four years at Stanford, including 304 as a freshman. That year he led the team to an undefeated season, during which he once scored 70 points in a two-game weekend.

While Luisetti's career reached its peak in the first invasion of Madison Square Garden, it was actually marked by a series of high points. He ripped a tie game with U.C.L.A. wide open with six baskets in the overtime period one night. He stole the ball five times in a game against California and scored each time, forcing the Golden Bears to abandon their offense and develop a new pattern. He once smothered Santa Clara with a 35-point performance, and on another occasion he delighted a packed San Francisco crowd with a one-handed 50-foot basket.

He was a reluctant hero, so modest that he had to be prodded into going for points. The first to insist that basketball was a team game, he was always trying to turn the spotlight over to his teammates. Besides, he enjoyed passing and dribbling as much as shooting.

Stanford trailed California by 15 points with six minutes to go in a game one night during Luisetti's sophomore year. Coach Johnny Bunn of the Indians stood up, cupped his hands and yelled, "For Pete's sake, shoot, Hank, shoot!"

So Hank started shooting—and scored 12 baskets before the final whistle, to give Stanford a 51–47 victory.

But perhaps his greatest performance came near the end of his college career in a game against Duquesne at Cleveland. It was forced on him by his teammates, Dinty Moore, Jack Calderwood, Art Stoefen and Howie Turner. All four of them refused to shoot, even when Luisetti passed the ball to them. Time after time, they threw it back, then moved out of scoring range. With nothing else to do with the ball, Hank had to aim for the basket.

He scored an unprecedented 50 points in a 92–27 Stanford victory. That was the night he needed a police escort to get back to his hotel.

Almost every conceivable honor was heaped on his head. He was a three-time All-American and twice the college player of the year. When the Helms Foundation picked an all-time All-American team, Luisetti was its first choice. He came within a whisker of beating out George Mikan for the player of the half century, named by *Sport Magazine* in 1951.

After he graduated, Luisetti became a San Francisco businessman, but he never lost interest in basketball. He played for the Phillips Oilers for a while, then, after World War II broke out, starred for several navy teams. After getting out of the service, he did considerable part-time coaching, following a spinal meningitis attack in the navy which ended his playing career. His 1951 Stewart Chevrolet team won the National A.A.U. championship. He still conducts a boys' basketball clinic every year for the San Francisco *Examiner*.

He could have made a career of coaching, but he refused all offers, including bids from both his alma mater and the Naval Academy. As late as 1948, when he was thirty-one, he turned down a fabulous offer to tour the country and exhibit the one-handed shots that made him famous.

In the trophy case at Palo Alto rest Ernie Nevers' football helmet, Ben Eastman's running spikes, Pop Warner's sweat shirt and Hank Luisetti's basketball jersey with a faded number seven on its back. The number has been permanently retired as a tribute to one of Stanford's greatest athletes and nicest guys.

3

BONES McKINNEY

W HEN Bones McKinney was six years old, a visitor patted his blond head and asked, "Sonny, what are you going to be when you grow up?"

"When I grow up," the youngster retorted, "I'm gonna be a big boy."

That was Bones' first known wisecrack. He's made a million of them since. Even though today he's the Wake Forest basketball coach and an ordained Baptist minister, he's still the clown prince of basketball. Within the bounds of decent behavior, for he is a fine gentleman, Bones Mc-Kinney will do anything for a laugh.

He really doesn't have to do very much, because his appearance and his name are funny enough. Bones is six feet, six inches tall, and when he was playing college and professional basketball, he was so thin that his backbone practically shook hands with his chest.

"He looks," an observer once remarked, "as though he never had a square meal in his life."

Bones has a long, sad face, which not only utterly obscures the merry spirit that lies behind it, but enables him to put on a masterful act on and about the basketball court. Shirley Povich of the Washington *Post and Times Herald* once pointed out that the initials of Bones' real name, Horace A. McKinney, spell "ham" and that nothing could have been more appropriate.

During his playing days, when he pleaded for justice from foul-calling referees, Bones lay on the floor and groaned, rested on his knees and pounded the floor in frustration and generally seemed on the verge of tears. Today, his histrionics on the bench when things go wrong with his Wake Forest team are even more picturesque. He squirms, smirks, pirouettes, waves his arms, points his fingers, holds his head, tears his thinning hair and dies a thousand deaths.

Bones didn't get his colorful nickname from his spare build, as many basketball fans think. He earned it by playing the part of a character called Beau Brummel Bones in a high school play. He welcomed the switch from Horace, although it was a transformation that horrified his mother. When friends phoned the house and asked for Bones, she invariably replied, "There's no one by that name here. If you wish to speak to Horace, I'll call him."

Bones grew up in Durham, North Carolina, where he starred on a high school basketball team that won 69 straight games. He entered North Carolina State on a basketball scholarship in 1940, and delighted observers with his antics on the court. He gave himself audible pep talks as he ran up and down, gravely thanked the referee every time a foul was called on him and elaborately checked the scorer's table whenever he sank a basket to make sure he got credit for it.

After marrying a co-ed, Bones went into the army, barely making it since his six feet, six inches was the exact height limit. When he got out, he transferred to North Carolina because he liked the basketball coach, Ben Carnevale. Thanks to Bones, the Tar Heels went to the N.C.A.A. finals, but lost the title to Oklahoma A.&M. when Bones fouled out of the game with 14 minutes to play.

After graduation in 1946, he left home one day in August, thinking he was headed for Chicago to sign with the Stags for $7500. But Bob Feerick, an army pal who played for the Washington Capitols, and Red Auerbach, the Caps' coach, intercepted him at the Washington railroad station.

"Forget Chicago," Feerick said. "Think of your wife and family. It's cheaper to phone them from Washington. Besides, the Caps will pay you as much as the Stags. Talk it over with Red."

Feerick then left Bones with Auerbach, which was like leaving a lamb with a leopard. Auerbach talked so fast that Bones signed a Caps' contract in the station washroom, and the Chicago train went on without him.

It wasn't long before Bones was convulsing fans all over the league. He hopped and skipped and simpered like a little girl as he dribbled. If the Caps were way ahead and nothing was at stake, he threw fouls with his back to the basket, often sinking them. When a player slid along the floor, Bones rushed toward him, yelling, "Out!" or "Safe!" If a vendor happened to be handy when Bones was forced off the floor, he grabbed popcorn or peanuts and walked through the crowd, hawking them.

He once landed on a woman's lap in Boston and posed there, patting her on the head, to the delight of everyone in the Garden, including the woman. Another time he wiped

the brow of a perspiring fan with a towel, loudly comment-
ing, "You need this more than I do."

In Detroit, he crashed into temporary seats and then
helped clear them off, ignoring the play at the other end of
the court. When he had finished that, he strolled all alone
to the opposing basket, then suddenly took a pass from
Freddy Scolari, which he casually dumped in.

When he missed a foul shot one night in Washington, he
took the ball to the referee and yelled, "Get a new ball.
This one's warped." When the referee refused, Bones appealed to the crowd, then rolled the ball along the floor
where it wobbled like a Mexican jumping bean. The referee
got a new ball.

The Caps went into a 17-game winning streak halfway
through the 1946–47 season, and Bones insisted on doing
everything exactly the same way. Day after day he ate the
same food, wore the same clothes, sat on the same place on
the bench, made his teammates file in and out of the locker
room in the same order and went to the same places he had
been on the previous trip into a town. A fan gave Bones an
Oriental doll which he named Yehudi. Each day everyone
on the team had to kiss the doll. When the streak ended,
Bones threw Yehudi into the crowd and ditched his whole
routine.

With all his clowning, Bones never forgot what the Caps
had hired him for, and he helped them to a fine season in
his rookie year. They won the Eastern Division title, and
both Bones and Feerick made the league All-Star team.

Both in Washington and Boston, where he played for the
Celtics after Auerbach became the coach, Bones flatly refused to enter an airplane.

"If the good Lord wanted me to fly, He'd have given me

wings," he said. "He gave me these big feet to run and walk on and to board trains with, and that's what I'm going to do."

One year the Celtics flew 30,000 miles without incident. Bones went everywhere by surface transportation and was involved in three minor train wrecks and a taxicab accident. But he still steadfastly refused to fly.

He decided to become a preacher in 1952, and he entered Southeastern Theological Seminary at Wake Forest, North Carolina, where he also helped Murray Greason coach the Wake Forest basketball team. Bones became the head coach in 1957 when Greason was made assistant athletic director.

He's an excellent basketball coach and a fine observer of promising young players. His 1961 and 1962 teams, sparked by All-American Len Chappell, won Atlantic Coast Conference titles, and his 1962 club took the Eastern Regional N.C.A.A. championship.

Still close to his old coach, McKinney scouts the South informally for Red Auerbach. It was Bones who discovered Sam Jones, an obscure college player who later became an outstanding Boston Celtics star.

Today Bones lives with his wife and six children in Winston-Salem, where Wake Forest College is now located. Besides coaching, he serves as assistant chaplain of the college, a job which he takes seriously and does well.

"If all I could ever be at Wake Forest was the basketball coach," he says, "I wouldn't stay here."

4

BILL SHARMAN

W HEN Bill Sharman was with the Boston Celtics, his roommate and close friend, Bob Cousy, called him the "all-American boy." Sharman was about as all-American as it is possible to get. Handsome, wholesome, popular, always cheerfully smiling, he was a hero wherever he went— in school, in the navy, in college and in professional ranks. He married his high school sweetheart, who was not only the head cheerleader but the most beautiful and most popular girl in town. They already had a family by the time Bill got out of the service and entered the University of Southern California.

There he pitched and played the outfield on the baseball team, and starred for four years in basketball. In 1950, his senior year, he actually *was* an All-American basketball player. He left college just before he got his degree to accept a $12,000 bonus for signing to play baseball in the Brooklyn Dodgers organization. When he was drafted for

Bill Sharman

basketball by the Washington Caps, he became a two-sport professional.

Finally, after he joined the Boston Celtics in 1951, he developed into the most accurate shooter in basketball history. As long as the game is played, Sharman will be the norm by which great shooters of the future are judged. There was never one like him, and there may never be another.

Ordinarily statistics are cold and dull, but the statistics on Sharman's fantastic foul shooting are fascinating. He set records that may live as long as basketball is played. Until he came along, no one had ever successfully converted 50 fouls in a row. Sharman did it three times, first in 1955, then in 1956–7 and finally in 1959. Each time, he broke his own record.

His 1959 performance of 56 straight, which now stands as the all-time N.B.A. mark, was under the pressure of playoffs. Anyone who has ever seen a playoff game can appreciate what that means. Sharman's feat was like sinking 18 long putts in a row during a National Open Golf Championship. It took a sure hand and nerves of iron.

During the ten years he played for the Celtics, Sharman led the N.B.A. in foul-shooting percentage seven times, and his lifetime average of 88.3 percent is another league record that is likely to stand the test of time. His nearest rival, Dolph Schayes of Syracuse, is more than four percentage points behind him.

Before leaving the field of statistics, it is interesting to note that Sharman scored 3143 fouls in 3557 attempts, which means he missed only 414 times in his N.B.A. career. His 1959 average of 93.2 percent is a league record. When he set it, Sharman broke his own mark of 90.5, set in 1957. Even in 1961, when he was thirty-four years old and his reflexes were no longer sharp, Sharman missed only 18 fouls in 228 tries for a 92.1 average. Schayes, who twice was 90.4, is the only other long-term N.B.A. player to hit with fouls more than 90 percent of the time in any one season.

Sharman didn't make seven All-League teams and play in eight All-Star games on his foul shooting alone. With the possible exception of Schayes, a forward and a much taller man, Sharman was the greatest outside shooter who ever lived. He was at his best from 15 to 35 feet away from the basket. When he retired from the N.B.A. at the end of the 1961 season, he stood eleventh in all-time floor shooting percentage, and the ten men ahead of him were all forwards. Sharman thus was the best shooting backcourt man in the game's history, and his lifetime mark of 42.3 percent was well ahead of many forecourt men.

What makes Sharman's records even more amazing is that, at six feet, one inch, he was one of the smallest men in pro basketball. Unlike the giants of the game, Sharman couldn't stuff the ball into the hoop or pick up many layups. He had to get almost all his points the hard way. In shooting, he depended entirely on accuracy.

He sank so many long shots that they couldn't possibly have been just lucky. Sharman practiced hours and hours from distances as far away as 50 feet. He didn't go for the backboard and hope for the ball to carom in—he aimed straight for the hoop. Most of his shots went in so cleanly that they didn't even touch the rim.

But his most spectacular shot was covered with horseshoes. He sank the longest recorded basket in history in the 1957 All-Star game at Boston when he hurled the ball in

from 70 feet away. Actually, it wasn't a good shot, but a
bad pass. Cousy was all alone near the basket, and Sharman
was trying to get the ball to him.

"It might not have been my biggest thrill," Sharman said
later, "but it was my biggest surprise."

His biggest thrill was the Celtics' first N.B.A. championship. After knocking on the door of the title for years, they
finally won in 1957, and Bill was one of the playoff stars.
That was the beginning of a streak that has made the
Celtics the Yankees of basketball. In the remaining years
that Sharman was with them, they captured three more
titles.

Despite his undeniable greatness, Sharman was always
overshadowed by others in his years at Boston. His backcourt partner, Bob Cousy, was the only little man in the
business who topped him. The Celtics' center, Bill Russell,
has consistently been the most valuable player in the league.
So, for the last five years of his career, Sharman was the
third man of a Russell-Cousy-Sharman triumvirate. And
before Russell came along, the Celtics had another great
center in Ed Macauley. He, too, overshadowed Sharman,
with the result that Bill was the junior partner in a
Macauley-Cousy-Sharman combination for the first five
years of his Boston career.

Yet no one ever depreciated Sharman's value. Red Auerbach, the Celtics' coach, never underestimated him, and has
often said that the Celtics wouldn't have been the great
team they were without him. They continued to win after
Sharman left only because other fine backcourt men were
developed, but, good as they were, they weren't as good as
Sharman in his prime.

He worked all his life on the feathery, one-handed shot

which was his stock-in-trade. Bill, born in Texas in 1926, grew up in Porterville, California. As a ten-year-old, his hero was Stanford's Hank Luisetti, the man who popularized the light, one-handed push shot. Sharman practiced it until he could sink it from all angles and from any reasonable distance.

But basketball wasn't his favorite game. From childhood, Sharman wanted to be a big league ballplayer. Everything he did was toward that aim. He liked all sports, but he loved baseball.

He was an amazing all-round athlete in high school. Before he was through, he won letters in baseball, football, basketball, track and tennis. He also dabbled in boxing and weight-lifting. In later years, he was just as versatile. He took up golf at thirty, and was shooting in the high 70's within three years.

If Sharman hadn't concentrated on baseball and basketball in college, he might have been an outstanding star in some other sport. He was undefeated in three years of high school tennis competition, and once played in the National Junior championships. He was also a fine T-formation quarterback as a schoolboy, a great passer, kicker and ball handler. As a track man, he put the shot, threw the javelin and ran the hurdles.

The busiest week of his life came at the end of his high school career in 1944. He graduated the day after his eighteenth birthday, and won the Central California tennis championship the day after that. He married Illeana Bough the following day, then joined the navy after a 24-hour honeymoon.

Sharman could have gone to any one of a dozen colleges on a football scholarship, but he decided to give up the game to protect his baseball future. He entered Southern California on the GI Bill of Rights in 1946, but three months later he had a basketball scholarship. As a junior, he became the second player in Pacific Coast Conference history to score 200 points in a season. The first had been his boyhood idol, Luisetti. A year later, Sharman broke Luisetti's record and made All-American.

Yet he never let his sights wander from baseball. He took the Dodgers' bonus and left school in March of 1950 because he and his wife had two children, and he needed the money more than the degree. When the Dodgers sent him to Pueblo in the Class A Western League, he considered his basketball career was over.

But he decided to try it when the Caps drafted him, so he joined them after the baseball season of 1950. The Caps folded halfway through the campaign, and Bill was assigned to Fort Wayne. Instead of reporting there, he told the owner, Fred Zollner, that he was giving up basketball, and went home to wait for the start of the next baseball season.

He had a good season at Fort Worth in 1951, and the Dodgers brought him up for a look just before the season ended. That was the nearest he got to the big leagues. The Dodgers were loaded with talent, and Sharman was just another outfielder as far as they were concerned. When they returned him to the minors in 1952, he reluctantly decided to quit.

By then his basketball career was secure. It had been up in the air for a while, because he was twice traded to the Celtics. The first deal was nullified on a technicality. He finally went along to Boston as a throw-in with a couple of other players for Charley Share.

Years later, Walter Brown, the Celtics owner, said, "We

drew Cousy's name out of a hat and took Sharman as an afterthought. How lucky can you get?"

Besides being a shooting genius, Sharman was one of the scrappiest athletes in the N.B.A. What he lacked in size, he made up in aggressiveness. In hassles which led to fisticuffs, he was a tough man to cross and a dangerous opponent in a fight.

Yet he never started trouble. He flared up only when somebody made things rough for him. Pro basketball had become a contact game by the time Sharman got into it, and careless hands, fists, elbows, shoulders or hips infuriated him. He was in some classic battles before he got through.

He once broke Andy Phillip's nose with a punch. Another time he knocked Noble Jorgenson, who stood six, ten, into the seats. Richie Guerin went on the shelf for half a season after breaking his hand hitting Sharman. In later years, Bill's fights were less frequent, largely because the rest of the league learned not to pick on him. The bigger men were easier to handle.

Sharman left the Celtics unexpectedly at the end of the 1961 season, when he accepted a three-year contract to coach Los Angeles in the newly formed American Basketball League. The team folded halfway through the 1962 season, and Bill ended up coaching Cleveland to a league title. The team folded a few months later, and Bill returned to California to become a college coach. With his playing days behind him, it looks as if he has a bright future as a teacher of the game that made him famous.

5

NAT HOLMAN

W HEN the college basketball betting scandals shocked the nation in February of 1951, nobody was more heartbroken than Nat Holman, the veteran City College of New York coach. Once the brain and nerve center of the fabulous Original Celtics, for over thirty years oracle of the sport he loved, recognized throughout the country as "Mr. Basketball," Holman had just reached new heights of success when the scandals broke.

Only a week before, he had proudly accepted *Sport Magazine*'s award as sport's man-of-the-year for piloting his underdog C.C.N.Y. team to an unprecedented sweep at Madison Square Garden in the spring of 1950. This club, made up largely of brilliant young sophomores, became the first team in history to win both the National Invitation Tournament and the N.C.A.A. championship in the same year.

By January, ugly rumors about "shaving points"—keeping the point difference between winners and losers within

a certain limit but not necessarily "throwing" the game—
were approaching a climax. Holman's answer to them was
an impatient "I'll stake my reputation on the integrity of
my boys."

Then the roof fell in. Three of Holman's boys were
among the first to be named by New York's District Attorney as "fixers," then four more followed. Holman, who
had always tried to teach decency, honesty and devotion to
duty along with basketball, never completely recovered
from the blow. He retired a year or two later and has lived
in comparative obscurity ever since.

But when he was in his heyday, nobody had more to say
about basketball and how the game should be played. For
over a generation, Holman was czar, interpreter, arbiter
and policymaker. He sat securely on a throne that was
partly of his own making, for he was no shrinking violet.
His self-assurance bordered on arrogance, but there was no
doubt of his intelligence. Holman was the man who put
brains into basketball. He transformed it from simply a
game to a scientific pastime.

Basketball itself was young when Holman began playing
it as a kid. The game was invented at Springfield College in
Massachusetts by Dr. James A. Naismith in 1891. Holman
was born on New York's East Side five years later, so the
man and the sport grew up together.

Holman played it on the streets as a kid, and in gymna-
siums as an adolescent and a young man. For a while, he
was a member of the New York Whirlwinds, one of the
country's first semi-pro teams. He never attended a formal
college but studied physical education at a school known
as Savage, then, in 1920, he became the C.C.N.Y. coach.

Less than a year later, Holman joined the Celtics. They
were a rag, tag and bobtail collection of fellows with a

Nat Holman

common devotion to basketball that amounted almost to a religion. They had been playing together as a team since 1914, but the success that made them legendary didn't come until 1922.

By then the club had seven basic members—Holman, Dutch Dehnert, Pete Barry, Horse Haggerty, Johnny Beckman, Chris Leonard and Joe Lapchick. Others filled in from time to time, but these seven were the backbone of the team. Except for Haggerty and Lapchick, who towered well over six feet, none was unusually tall.

The Celtics, greatest team of their time (some diehards still insist it was the greatest of all time), were neither the richest nor the best-dressed basketball team in the country, but they were far and away the most successful. They took on all comers, and when they couldn't get teams to go to New York, they traveled east, south and west in day coaches seeking competition. For seven years, they won over a hundred games a year, and in their worst seasons, they lost less than twenty.

They devised plays and formations that became standard maneuvers in basketball—indeed, some still are. Holman was the genius of the gang. He figured out the moves, then showed his teammates how to execute them. In a sense, he was the Bob Cousy of his day, for his ball handling was magnificent. He was the best passer, the best faker, the smartest player in the game. He could almost thread a needle with the ball, which he threw without a spin, so that it floated easily into the arms of the receiver. A master at drawing fouls, Holman could recoil from an opponent so convincingly that he appeared to be hit when there hadn't even been any physical contact.

With the center jump after each basket and 20-minute halves, scores were never very high. The Celtics kept the totals even lower by freezing the ball. They could kill half a period by passing it back and forth among themselves. Holman insisted that they shoot only for sure baskets. As a result, they often won games with as little as fifteen points.

This was the basketball he taught his C.C.N.Y. teams, and it was copied all over the East. But in the West, a new type of game was being devised, a game of running and shooting, of taking chances in going for the basket. The set shot which was basic with Holman was augmented by shots from all angles. Scores in the West were much higher than in the East, and some philistines were hinting that perhaps it was a better game.

The first big test came during Christmas vacation of 1936, when Stanford, sparked by Hank Luisetti and his spectacular one-handed shot, whipped mighty Long Island University at Madison Square Garden. Holman was not impressed, not even after Stanford trounced his own C.C.N.Y. team a year later.

"I'll quit before I teach one-handed shooting to my team," he said.

It took him ten years to admit he was wrong. Not until 1947 did he join the rest of the crowd. By then, the game had almost gone by him.

"Holman," said his detractors, "is all through."

But Holman, severe, conservative, unbending, devoted to the memory of his beloved Celtics, suddenly accepted the challenge of the times. It was big news when he scrapped the past and began teaching the game of the future. He had capitulated at last—and observers wondered if he had waited too long.

Within two years, he gave them their answer. C.C.N.Y. opened the 1949–50 season by winning 13 of its first 15 games. Holman's team of sophomores was the talk of basketball, especially after it broke St. John's 12-game winning streak. Then it started to fold, but the coach pulled it together again, and the team earned its N.I.T. bid.

The man whose basketball philosophy had always been based on smooth, well-organized, low-scoring games sat on the bench during the N.I.T. games of 1950 and watched his club beat San Francisco 65–46, Kentucky 89–50, Duquesne 62–52, and Bradley 69–61, to win the tournament. A week later, the game's great conservative watched the same team on the same floor win the N.C.A.A. title by beating Ohio State 56–55, and North Carolina State 78–73, then scoring a second smashing victory over Bradley 71–68.

It was the grand climax, one of the great triumphs of basketball history. The deposed king was back on his throne, once again master of all he surveyed. The Boswells of the game who had ignored him now flocked around for statements and opinions, and the experts who had thought he clung to the past too long listened to what he had to say.

They found a new Nat Holman, not the austere martinet of previous years, but a rather warm man who wanted to unbend, to be out of the freezer into which he had locked himself for so many years. Marriage, the change from the old to the new, and the great double victory of his team had humanized the man. Holman was still the oracle, but now he was willing to concede that others might have known something about the game too.

He was ready to compromise—ready to give credit to the new, even at the expense of the old.

"Kids today are better shots than in my time," he said. "They have better control of the ball with one hand than we had with two."

This from the man who threatened to quit before teaching one-handed basketball!

But he refused to try to compare any team, amateur or professional, with the Celtics so close to his heart.

"Basketball is altogether different from twenty-five years ago," he once declared. "You can't compare players of different eras."

Perhaps Nat Holman wasn't the greatest basketball coach who ever lived, but he was very, very close. It's too bad he never coached in the pro leagues as we know them today. It's possible that he could even have taught the mighty Boston Celtics, namesakes of the team that meant so much to him, a thing or two.

6

ED MACAULEY

THEY called him Easy Ed Macauley because he did everything so effortlessly and never got excited. He looked like a will-o'-the-wisp gliding down the court, and when he shot a basket, he handled the ball as though it were a soufflé. Of all the great basketball players—and he was one of them—Easy Ed had the lightest touch.

He had brains, too, and speed and grace and height. All he lacked was strength, and if he had had that he might have been the greatest of them all. But Macauley had only 190 pounds to distribute the length of his six feet, eight and one half inches. He was so skinny that he brought out the mother instinct in every woman who watched him play. Against all those big, rugged men in the N.B.A., it didn't seem possible that he could survive a game.

In ten years he survived 641 of them. When he retired to coach the St. Louis Hawks in November of 1958, he was the fourth leading scorer of N.B.A. history. At the time, his 11,234 points—an average of 17.5 a game—left him behind only three of basketball's immortals, Dolph

Ed Macauley

Schayes, Bob Cousy and George Mikan. Others have passed him since, but Macauley's place is secure; he will always belong in the top flight.

He first won national fame at St. Louis University, where he was an All-American in his junior year, but he reached his peak with the Boston Celtics. He was their big man for six years, and ranked as the top center in the league for three of them. And, along with Cousy and Coach Red Auerbach, Macauley helped put professional basketball over in Boston.

The game was tottering before the three arrived in the Hub in 1950. The 1949–50 Celtics finished last in the league's Eastern Division and Boston fans, who didn't know much about basketball anyhow, were caring less each year. There was every indication that Walter Brown, the Celtics' owner, would either have to fold his club or take it somewhere else.

He had lost a bundle on it and was in hock up to his ears. Then, at the suggestion of Lou Pieri, his partner, he hired Auerbach. The first thing the new coach said was, "We've got to get a good big man or we're dead."

Macauley had just finished his first season as a pro. The St. Louis Bombers had paid him $15,000, a record salary for a rookie up to that time, and Easy Ed had had a good year. But it wasn't good enough to save the Bombers. They finished last in the Central Division, and were forced to fold.

Ned Irish, president of the New York Knickerbockers, quickly tried to buy the franchise for the sole purpose of getting Macauley. His offer of $25,000 would probably have been accepted, but Auerbach blocked the deal. Since the Celtics had finished last in their division, he demanded first choice of the St. Louis players. The league agreed with him, and Macauley went to Boston.

Easy Ed had a tremendous season, the first of several. He made the All-League team, and was named the outstanding player in the All-Star game, which the East club won. He scored 1384 points during the year, finishing third, behind only George Mikan and Alex Groza. Most important of all, he helped rescue the Celtics for Brown and Boston.

Actually, their 1950–51 season was nothing to get excited about. They finished second and lost to the Knicks in the first round of the playoffs. But, for the first time, the fans began to show some interest. Before the season was over, they were coming out to see Cousy and Macauley, and the two put on a show worth watching.

In one of their favorite maneuvers, Cousy would take the ball down the court on a fast break, and Easy Ed would lope along behind him. As he got into enemy territory, Cousy would stop and, without looking, drop the ball over his shoulder. Macauley would be there to take it, then, with a neat flick of his wrist, he would flip it through the hoop.

Sometimes Ed would whisper "right" or "left," so that Cousy would know which side might be more convenient, but most of the time the boys pulled the stunt without any prompting. Macauley got a lot of baskets that way and the customers loved it. But he scored more in conventional ways and, long before the season ended, Boston's new basketball fans realized that in Easy Ed they had one of the great stars of the league.

After Bill Sharman joined the Celtics as Cousy's backcourt partner in 1951, Boston's big two became a big three. For five years they made the team a constant threat for the league title. The two little men provided the color, finesse and fireworks, while Easy Ed provided the points. Year after year, the club was the best drawing card in the league. They won no titles, but they made friends and influenced people all over the circuit.

Macauley was consistently among the league's scoring leaders—fourth in 1952 and again in 1953, then third in 1954. He hit for over 1000 points all six years he was with the Celtics, pouring in 1402 in 1953, his best year. During that season, he set a league record for one game by scoring 46 points against Minneapolis. A year later, he sank 462 field goals in 950 attempts for a record average of .486. These marks have been broken since, but so have most basketball records.

Easy Ed seldom fouled out. He could be rough, and sometimes was, but he rarely got hit with the six personal fouls that send a man to the bench for the duration. During one stretch of four years, from 1952 to 1956, he didn't once get banished.

Besides being a star, Macauley was one of the most popular men in the league. Cheerful and friendly, as well as deeply religious, he had the respect of friend and foe alike. When Cousy formed the Players' Association to insure better conditions for the athletes, Macauley was his strongest supporter and did much to help make it work.

League executives respected his opinion as much as players did. In 1954 the league was in trouble because the rules permitted too much stalling. Crucial games were turned into travesties as teams protected leads by holding the ball, not daring to shoot for fear of losing it. It was a throwback to the early days of the game, and the customers began staying away in droves.

Dan Biasone, owner of the Syracuse club, suggested a time limit for freezing the ball, but there was such a storm of protest from the rest of the league that it seemed to have little chance of going through. Then one day, at a luncheon in Boston, Macauley stood up and said, "Make us shoot the ball within a set number of seconds, and you'll see a better game."

That broke the log jam. One after another, players and coaches fell into line, and that summer the 24-second rule was put into effect. With the exception of Biasone, Macauley probably had more to do with its passage than any other individual.

Unhappily, Boston fans and sports writers eventually began to show impatience with the Celtics' tendency always to be bridesmaids but never brides. They were the most consistent second-place finishers in the N.B.A., then bowed to somebody else somewhere along the playoffs. Next to Auerbach, the coach, the biggest target of criticism was the biggest man, Easy Ed Macauley.

His trouble was his inability to grab many rebounds. Great as he was from the floor and at the foul line, he couldn't compete with men fifty and seventy-five pounds heavier in battles for the ball off the backboards. The Celtics out scored the other clubs every year, but they were also the easiest to score against. Without a good rebound man, they would never win, and no one knew this better than Auerbach.

Macauley was the man on the spot, but there was little he could do about it. His forte was putting the ball through the hoop. Hard as he tried—and he tried very hard indeed —he had no more chance of becoming a rebound star than Tom Thumb of becoming a layup expert. He just wasn't built right.

As the years passed, Macauley set up business interests in St. Louis, where he continued to make his home. By 1956, it was necessary for him to spend more time there. He told the Celtics that he would have to retire from the game unless they traded him to the Hawks.

They made a historic deal, sending Easy Ed and Cliff Hagan to St. Louis in return for the draft rights on Bill Russell. It helped both teams, for Macauley and Hagan sparked the Hawks to a league championship and several Western Division titles, while Russell was the man the Celtics needed to become consistent winners.

With others available for rebounding, Easy Ed fitted perfectly into the Hawks' scheme of things. Bob Pettit was their big man and, with the pressure off his own thin shoulders, Macauley had one of his best seasons. He scored 1187 points, and helped the Hawks win their first Western Division championship. They lost the playoffs to the Celtics, but they carried the battle all the way to the limit of seven games before bowing in overtime.

The next year, Easy Ed, then thirty, had slowed up perceptibly, but he still scored over 1000 points for the ninth straight year. The Hawks again won their division title, and that time they went on to take the N.B.A. crown too. They were the last team to crack the Celtics' monopoly on the championship, for Boston followed with four titles in a row.

Macauley came back for the 1958–59 season with some reservations, for his business and personal affairs were taking up more and more of his time. He finally decided to play, but knew it would be his last campaign. Six weeks after it began, he was faced with a new problem.

His alma mater, St. Louis University, wanted him to return as basketball coach and athletic director, and he was mulling that over in his mind. Then, in November, the

Hawks' owner, Ben Kerner, suddenly offered him a three-year contract at $20,000 a year to become coach and executive vice-president of the team.

Kerner was notorious for firing coaches. Since the beginning of the 1956–57 season, only two years before, the Hawks had had four, Red Holzman, Slater Martin, Alex Hannum and Andy Phillip. Hannum had failed to survive after winning the N.B.A. title, and Phillip had been around only a few weeks.

Macauley took the job. He lasted two years, winning the Western Division championship both times, but failing both times to stop the Celtics' march to the N.B.A. title. The second failure was too much for Kerner. He paid Easy Ed off, and that was the end of Macauley's pro basketball career.

When it was all over, Macauley shrugged his narrow shoulders and said with a rueful grin, "I guess I should have expected this. At least, I had a good time while it lasted."

So did the St. Louis fans. They loved the tall, skinny man with the soft touch and the friendly smile, and they were sorry to see him go. That was the way everyone else felt about Easy Ed. He left the game just the way he entered it —without an enemy in the world.

7

JOE LAPCHICK

Basketball coaches are probably the sports world's worst "bleeders." They suffer pangs of anguish in every game. In most cases, they make no attempt to keep their feelings to themselves. They jump up and down on the bench, scream at officials and work themselves up into a lather when things go wrong. Even when things go right, they sit on a tinderbox of anxiety, wondering how long it will last.

The fans share every morsel of grief with the outwardly bleeding coach who suffers in anything but silence. But a select few bleed inwardly, often sitting with apparent calm until the tension becomes more than they can stand. Then, sometimes long before the game ends, they blow up.

The classic prototype of the inwardly bleeding coach is Joe Lapchick, who sandwiched nine suffering years with the New York Knickerbockers between two tours of duty at St. John's University. At sixty-one, the towering Lapchick, who stands six feet, five inches, is one of the oldest

active coaches in the game. Considering what he puts himself through with each contest, it's a miracle that he's alive
at all.

Lapchick, who takes every defeat as a personal affront,
loses fifteen pounds a season, and he can't spare one of
them. When a campaign is over, he looks like a candidate
for the graveyard, a long toothpick of a man with new
wrinkles on his face, new sadness in his eyes and new gray
in what's left of his hair.

He once wrote a magazine piece, in collaboration with
W. C. Heinz, called "Each Game I Die." Never did a story
have a more appropriate title. The piece appeared in
Collier's in 1954, when Lapchick was the Knickerbockers'
coach. Now that he is back at St. John's, where he first
began coaching in 1936, it is still appropriate. Lapchick
dies almost as many deaths with college players as he did
with the pros.

"You die because you have so little control over what
happens," he once said. "This is a humiliating business.
There are no geniuses in coaching. The players make the
coach. The coach who thinks his coaching is more important than his talent is an idiot."

Lapchick was being overly modest. Few coaches mean
as much to their men as he does to his. He is one of basketball's real coaching geniuses, for his teams have won scores
of tough games against better opponents. A gentle man
whose sad exterior hides a heart of almost unbelievable
warmth, Lapchick has the ability to inspire others to rise
above themselves. For both positive and negative reasons,
even his mediocre teams sometimes play like champions.
From a positive standpoint, they want to win for Lapchick.
From a negative one, they can't stand the sight of his grief
when they lose.

Stomach cramps, which plague Lapchick from the beginning to the end of every basketball campaign, often send him to his bed in mid-season, and sometimes to the hospital. When he had a particularly vicious attack a few years ago, his doctor told him, "The trouble with you is that you're suffering day after day what the average person suffers once or twice in a lifetime."

It's quite true that Lapchick suffers practically a shock a day during the basketball season. Sometimes his traumatic experiences are as jarring off the court as on it. Typical was his reaction to a 1949 decision to trade Tommy Byrnes to the Baltimore Bullets in a deal that brought big Connie Simmons to the Knickerbockers.

Byrnes had broken in with the Knicks in 1947, just before Lapchick started coaching them. The young man had always lived in the New York area, and Lapchick knew he didn't want to leave. Because of this, it took Joe several days to agree to the trade and several more to break the news to Byrnes. By then, he was in such a state of nervous exhaustion that he had to go to the hospital for a week.

In 1944, when Lapchick's St. John's team played De Paul in the finals of the National Invitation Tournament, Lapchick watched in horror as De Paul, led by George Mikan, went into a first-half lead. But when Mikan fouled out five minutes after the second half began, St. John's began a comeback and was soon in front. When Lapchick realized his team was going to win, he fainted on the bench, and was out for eight minutes.

During the heat of the 1952 professional campaign, the Knickerbockers once blew a lead at Fort Wayne, and the Pistons pulled the game out in the last two seconds. Lapchick walked off the Knicks' bench like a man in a trance. His gait was stiff-legged, his eyes glazed, his lips a thin line and his face chalk white. He went blindly to the locker room, where he promptly collapsed. That time he spent three days in the hospital.

On another occasion, after the Knicks piled up a 12-point lead with five minutes to go, then lost the game in the final seconds, Joe walked off the floor with tears streaming down his cheeks. Later he couldn't remember having cried, but agreed that it was possible that he might do anything under such distressing conditions.

In Boston, he once threw off his coat, systematically tore out the lining and had the sleeves half ripped off before he realized what he was doing. He smashed a chair against the wall in the Knicks' dressing room in Chicago. Once, in utter frustration over an adverse decision, Joe picked up the water bucket, threw it high in the air and didn't budge as it drenched him coming down.

All through each season, he slept an average of an hour or two a night and ate so poorly that his digestive system went haywire. After a thorough physical examination, a doctor said, "Joe, there's nothing organically wrong with you, but I can't understand why."

Lapchick has been crazy about basketball since he started to play it as a twelve-year-old in 1912. Born and brought up in Yonkers, he used to practice by aiming a cap stuffed with paper at a point on the sloping roof of the tenement house where he lived. At fourteen he was playing for the Hollywood Inn team of Yonkers, and a year later was collecting five dollars a game playing for a team known as the Bantams.

He never finished high school. He had a regular job as a machinist before he was sixteen, making fifteen dollars a week. But during the basketball season, he collected as much as forty dollars a week playing for four or five different professional teams.

By the time he was twenty, Joe was as famous for his height as his basketball ability. At six feet, five, he was one of the tallest men in sports, for it wasn't until years later that the really big men began playing basketball. Joe was in demand because it was the age of the center jump, and the bigger the center the better the team was likely to be.

Inevitably Joe became a member of the fabulous Original Celtics. He joined the team in 1922 and played with this legendary group for five years. After that, he drifted around from one professional team to another, landing back with the Celtics in 1930. That team was not as good as its predecessor, but it was good enough to attract attention wherever it went, and Joe was its big wheel.

Much to his amazement, he was offered the job of basketball coach at St. John's in 1936. "Imagine," he said later, "me, a machinst with no education, getting a job like that. I wasn't even sure how to talk to college kids."

All he had to do was talk in his natural voice. Lapchick is soft-spoken and sincere, and the kids loved him almost on sight. He taught them what he had learned in his years with the Celtics, and they swore by him. St. John's, which had never before had a winning season, won thirteen and lost seven that year. From then on, they never lost more than seven games in any one year under Lapchick.

Joe spent eleven years at St. John's, during which seven of his teams qualified for the N.I.T. games. It won the championship in 1943 and 1944 to become the only team in history to capture the tournament two seasons in a row.

When, after returning to St. John's years later, Lapchick built up another winner, he became the first coach ever to win the tourney three times.

He left St. John's to coach the Knickerbockers in 1947, and the next nine years were a nightmare for him. At no time did he have an outstanding team, yet he always managed to get it into the playoffs. His Knickerbockers reached the finals three times, and twice lost the N.B.A. championship in the last seconds of the deciding game.

The grueling 72-game professional schedule and the pressure-packed playoffs that followed ripped Lapchick apart. By 1956 he couldn't take it any more. He resigned just before the end of the season, then gladly accepted an offer to return to St. John's.

The college, which was in the process of moving from its old campus in Brooklyn to a new one in Jamaica, had dropped basketball after the gambling scandals of 1950. With little material and almost no student interest at all, Joe had to start from scratch. It took him only two years to build up his N.I.T. winner, which generated campus enthusiasm as red-hot as ever.

"The game still tears me up," Lapchick said not long ago. "But now I go through it only 25 times a year instead of 72. Still, I'm convinced I'll go to my grave a younger man because of basketball."

Everyone who knows Lapchick or has ever had anything to do with him fervently hopes that that day will be a long time coming.

8

SLATER MARTIN

SLATER (DUGIE) MARTIN was the last of the great truly little men in pro basketball. There are still a few considered "little" but, unlike Martin, all are over six feet tall. Martin, a diminutive bundle of dynamite from Texas, stood only five feet, ten inches, yet held his own in the company of giants for 11 years. When he retired at thirty-four in 1960, he left the legacy of a bulldog, for every man who ever played against him remembers him as the toughest little guy in the N.B.A.

He once squared off with Wally Dukes, the seven-foot center of the Detroit Pistons, and it took three men to pull him away. He was the only man who could hold the fabulous Bob Cousy in check with a fair degree of consistency. Bill Sharman, Cousy's former Boston Celtics backcourt partner, once said of Martin, "I'm glad to see him guard Cousy. I only get him when I'm hot."

Other backcourt men all over the league felt the same way. They hated to face Cousy and Sharman, but Martin sometimes scared them more. "The trouble is," one said, "he never lets you alone. He's a perpetual motion machine. I don't know where he gets all the energy."

Martin, being short and so near-sighted that he had to wear contact lenses, had a ready answer. "I exist on energy in this game," he said. "I haven't got much else. And I learned a long time ago that if you keep running, the guy against you is gonna get tired."

Nobody was ever sure what made Martin great. He was too small to cope with the huge stars of the game, yet he often played them to a standstill. He wasn't considered an outstanding shooter, yet he ranked eleventh in playoff scoring and was among the top 25 all-time scorers when he retired. He didn't seem to be an unusual ball-handler, yet he controlled the ball as much as anyone whenever he was on the court.

A close observer remarked one day, "Dugie is the Eddie Stanky of basketball. He's too small to play, he can't shoot, he's not a fast runner and he doesn't do tricks with the ball, yet he's one of the greatest clutch players and defensive stars the game has ever seen."

Although he played on four championship teams in seven years at Minneapolis, Martin was never really appreciated until he went to St. Louis in 1956. He helped transform the Hawks from a so-so team into the best in the Western Division, and he was a big factor in the world's championship they won over the Celtics in 1958.

"I've never seen a tougher competitor in the clutch," Cousy said later. "He simply refused to let us beat him."

Martin got so much satisfaction out of winning that he never cared about his own performance. In the final game of the 1957 playoffs, which went into two overtime periods before the Celtics beat the Hawks, Martin held Cousy to two baskets in 20 shots and outscored the Boston star, 23 to 12. But in later years, he refused to talk about it.

"I want to forget that game," he said. "We lost."

He didn't do anywhere nearly as good a job on Cousy in the last game of the 1958 playoffs, for he collected only 4 points to Cousy's 15, but his face lights up when anyone mentions it. "That was a great game," says Martin. "We won."

Once the season began, his dedication to basketball was absolute. He ate, drank, slept, dreamt and lived the game from the beginning of the season to the end. He talked of nothing else until the last playoff battle was over.

Buddy Blattner, the radio announcer traveling with the Hawks a few years ago, often roomed with Martin. The team got into Boston at three o'clock one morning, and Blattner immediately fell asleep. Three hours later he woke up and saw Martin pacing the floor. When Blattner asked what was wrong, Dugie replied, "Nothing. I'm thinking about Cousy."

"At six o'clock in the morning?" Blattner asked.

"I'm always thinking about Cousy," Martin said.

Martin always thought ahead, too. For that reason, he hated to stay around locker rooms after games. Asked why he got dressed and out so quickly, he answered, "Why stick around? If we lose, I don't want to hear any more about it. If we win, I want to think about the next game."

Martin never collected what he was worth until he left Minneapolis. He had constant salary disputes with the Lakers' front office, which failed to give him what he considered a decent salary even after he first made the All-Star team in 1954.

The Lakers' big man was George Mikan, followed in importance and salary range by Vern Mikkelsen and Jim Pollard. By the time these men were paid, there wasn't much left for anyone else. During the seven years that Martin played for the Lakers, he held out at least four times before signing his contract.

Once, a Laker executive, in answer to Martin's demands for more money, sneered, "We can win with Mikan, Mikkelsen, Pollard and two bellhops. Who needs you?"

In 1956, Martin held out the night of the opening game of the season, finally signing for $9000. Not having had a moment of practice with the rest of the team, he sat on the bench at the start of the game, against the Hawks at Minneapolis. By the end of the first period, the Hawks were ahead, thanks to 15 points by Frank Selvy. Johnny Kundla, the Lakers' coach, turned to Martin and asked, "Can you stop him, Dugie?" When Martin nodded, Kundla sent him into the game, and he held Selvy to three points in the remaining 36 minutes.

Bob Davies of the Rochester Royals was one of the top backcourt men of the game. Martin once actually shut him out, the only time in 16 years Davies failed to score a basket from the floor.

Martin was born in a town that went out of existence when his family moved. There was nothing in Elmina, Texas, except his grandfather's general store. The family went to Houston, 70 miles away, when Dugie was two. By then, everyone called him by that nickname. It was given to him by his grandfather after Dugan's Tavern, then featured in the Mutt and Jeff comic strip.

Dugie was always a great all-round athlete. He played

baseball, basketball and football at Jefferson Davis High School, and he even did some amateur boxing. The basketball team won two straight state championships in Martin's junior and senior years.

At the University of Texas, Martin became the highest basketball scorer in west Texas history. During a three-year career interrupted by service in the navy in World War II, Dugie piled up 1140 points. When he scored 49 against Texas Christian, he set a Southwest Conference record that stood for years.

By the time he joined the Lakers in 1949, Martin was married and had a family. He could have made more money doing something else, but he was so eager to play pro basketball he accepted a low salary just for the opportunity. With all the grief this led to, it was a decision he never regretted.

"I wanted to play basketball for a living," he said later. "I wouldn't have been happy doing anything else, even though I might have made more money."

Dwarfed by Mikan and the other big men of the mighty Lakers, who won four titles in five years, Martin seldom had much chance to stand out offensively. His biggest night came at the end of the 1952 season when, with Mikan, Mikkelsen and Pollard all well covered in the final playoff game against the New York Knickerbockers, Martin scored 32 points to clinch the championship for the Lakers.

His refusal to sign until the last minute of the 1956 season made it almost imperative for the Lakers to trade him, for neither he nor they were happy. Ben Kerner, the Hawks' owner, made a good offer for him, but the Lakers didn't want Martin in the same division with them. They sent him to the Knicks for Wally Dukes. Three weeks later, New York traded him to the Hawks for Willie Naulls, so Martin ended up in St. Louis anyhow.

That was the end of his financial troubles and the beginning of the Hawks' golden era. When the season was over, Kerner said, "Martin saved the franchise. I'd have gone broke without him."

Bob Pettit, the Hawks' great center, put it another way. "Dugie gave us the leadership we needed. He was the glue that held us together."

Kerner made Dugie the Hawks' coach soon after he arrived in St. Louis, but Martin hated the job. After one game, he delegated authority to Alex Hannum, his roommate, then resigned a week later. Hannum succeeded him and took the Hawks through the 1957 playoffs and the 1958 championship.

The only thing that caught up with Martin was age. He limped through the 1959–60 season, hampered by injuries which wouldn't have bothered him five years before. He quit when the playoffs were over, ending one of the game's most remarkable careers.

Basketball buffs will never forget him. He was the little man's little man, a David who spent eleven years cutting down Goliaths.

9

ADOLPH RUPP

ADOLPH RUPP is the proudest, most demanding college basketball coach in the United States, and he's also probably the greatest. In 32 years, his University of Kentucky teams won nearly 700 games and lost less than 140. Four of them captured national championships, 18 won Southern Conference titles and two became basketball legends.

So did Rupp. This sixty-year-old disciplinarian, precise, blunt and thorough, is an absolute perfectionist. When Sid Cohen, one of his recent stars, finished practicing foul shots one afternoon, Rupp asked, "How many, son?"

"Twenty-three out of twenty-five," Cohen said proudly.

"What happened to the other two?" Rupp demanded.

The Kentucky coach, known as the Baron wherever basketball is played, has been goading youths with questions like that for more than three decades. By refusing to settle for anything short of perfection, he has not only been a consistent winner but he has developed 19 All-American

Adolph Rupp

players. He has also sent hundreds of young men into the world with a healthy respect for authority.

His old grads hold him in awe and affection. They frequently return to Lexington to visit the man who once ruled their lives with the strictest hand most of them ever knew. Many have brought their children to meet him and some are now bringing their grandchildren.

Rupp is systematic to the point of fussiness, but he feels this is the only way to operate. "Basketball is a game of rhythm," he says, "and rhythm can only be accomplished by constant repetition. This is why I insist that everything be done over and over and over again, for perfection can be achieved in no other way."

The thoroughness of Rupp's approach can best be appreciated by the fact that he has movies taken of every practice session. Not even in football, where coaches are considered the fussiest of all, are movies taken in practice. Football coaches study game movies taken once a week. Rupp studies practice movies every day.

He is in his office at exactly seven-thirty in the morning. After a preliminary look at his correspondence, which is prodigious, Rupp and his long-time assistant, Harry Lancaster, go over their movies and plan the day's work. Before the morning is over, both have pages of notes to pore over.

Practice begins at exactly three-fifteen P.M., and the boys work at warm-up shooting for precisely half an hour. On the dot of three-forty-five, they begin twenty minutes of offensive drill, and follow that with twenty minutes of defensive work. Then they scrimmage, and end up with foul-shooting practice.

Few outsiders have ever witnessed a practice session, for Rupp insists this be private. He orders the doors locked, and no one is allowed in or out. In answer to protests by reporters and other parties who might be interested in watching his men at work, Rupp snaps, "I'm a teacher. I don't want people coming in and out during my classes."

Practice is held in the Memorial Coliseum, the "house that Rupp built." This is a tremendous concrete structure erected in 1950 at a cost of four million dollars. Although it has a seating capacity of 12,000 and can hold another 2000 standees, it often isn't big enough to accommodate all the fans who want to see the Wildcats in action.

Rupp considers the building his personal property. He refuses to let anything interfere with his basketball practice. Artur Rubinstein, the pianist, who had a concert sched-

uled at the Coliseum one night, requested silence while rehearsing during the afternoon. Just as he sat down at the
piano, Rupp led his basketball players to the floor.

An official stopped the coach and said, "Mr. Rubinstein
is rehearsing. You can't use the Coliseum today."

"We can't use it?" Rupp bellowed. "Listen—when Mr.
Rubinstein plays here tonight he can miss a hundred notes
and nobody will know the difference. But we're playing
Louisiana State tomorrow night and if one of my boys
misses a foul shot the whole world will know."

The team practiced and Mr. Rubinstein had to go somewhere else to rehearse. That was the first and last time anyone ever tried to keep Rupp out of the Coliseum.

Until 1951, when the reputation of one of his greatest
teams was tarnished by gambling disclosures, Kentucky was
a regular visitor to New York's Madison Square Garden.
After Kentucky's part in the scandals came to light, the
college was suspended for a year by the National Collegiate
Athletic Association. Rupp bitterly protested the move, and
it is still a subject of controversy in Kentucky. When the
Wildcats were reinstated, they continued to play all comers,
but they never returned to New York. To this day, Rupp
feels the temptations of big city basketball are too great for
college kids from the hinterlands.

The scandal-ridden team was one of the greatest college
clubs ever put together. Known as the "Wonder Five," it
captured two successive national championships and formed
the backbone of the 1948 United States Olympic basketball
team. At Kentucky, the team won 36 and lost 3 in 1947
and won 25 and lost 3 a year later.

When the gambling disclosures were first made in 1951,
Rupp said, "They couldn't touch any of my boys with a
ten-foot pole." A week later, three of them confessed. Of

the "Wonder Five," only Wah-Wah Jones and Cliff Barker weren't involved in the betting coups. Rupp's reaction was cold anger. To this day, he rarely mentions the men who took money for keeping scores within a point spread.

Rupp's favorite team is his amazing 1953–54 club, which was undefeated in winning another national championship for him. This outfit, spearheaded by Lou Tsioropoulos, Frank Ramsey and Cliff Hagan, won 25 straight games. Two are still professional stars, Ramsey with the Boston Celtics and Hagan with the St. Louis Hawks.

Both still run, shoot, cut and pass the way Rupp taught them in their college days. Red Auerbach, the Boston Celtics coach, says of Rupp's graduates, "They're the best-coached kids to come to the pros. They don't make many mistakes, and they don't take wild shots as so many other rookies do. They only shoot when they have a chance to score."

The year after the undefeated season, the Wildcats rolled up seven more victories before their winning streak was stopped at 32 games. The team that halted the string was an underdog Georgia Tech five, and to add insult to injury, the deed was done in Kentucky's own Coliseum. After the game, Rupp told his boys, "There have been two great catastrophes in our time. One was Pearl Harbor. The other was tonight."

His team went on to win 16 of its remaining 18 games for a season's record of 23 and 3. This gave Rupp the fantastic total of 48 victories in 51 games for the two seasons combined.

The Baron coaches because he loves it, not because he has to. Actually, he is one of the wealthiest and most respected men in the sports world. He has a 1000-acre ranch near Lexington, where he raises Hereford cows and grows tobacco. In 1949 he was named Kentucky's outstanding citizen, and he has won many other honors beyond the field of sports.

A prominent Mason, Rupp once was included in a group designated the ten outstanding Shriners of the year. Some of those named with him were President Harry Truman, Captain Eddie Rickenbacker, General Hap Arnold, General Claire Chennault, the poet Edgar Guest and the composer Sigmund Romberg.

Born on a Kansas farm in 1902, Rupp put himself through the University of Kansas working in the wheat fields and as a janitor. He also played basketball for Coach Phog Allen, and was a member of the national championship Kansas team of 1923. Rupp later got a master's degree at Columbia, then became a high school teacher-coach. He accepted the job of coaching basketball at Kentucky only because he thought it would lead to something better later.

He has been at Lexington ever since. Today, he is as much a Kentucky institution as Happy Chandler, mint juleps and the Kentucky Derby. He even talks with the soft drawl of the South which has been his home for so long. And he keeps on winning so consistently that other coaches in the Southern Conference can't wait until he retires.

A few years ago there was a false rumor that Rupp had died. A Southern Conference coach known to be antagonistic to the Baron told a friend that he was planning to go to Lexington for the funeral.

"Say, that's a real nice gesture," the friend said.

"Real nice gesture, my foot," the coach retorted. "I just want to make sure he's dead."

Rupp wasn't, of course. And before he's through, he's almost certain to win several more Conference titles and perhaps another national championship or two.

10

TOMMY HEINSOHN

I**F** T**OMMY** H**EINSOHN** had played for any team other than the Boston Celtics, he would have been hailed as a super-star long ago. But the Celtics were already knee-deep in stars when Heinsohn joined them in 1956. Bob Cousy and Bill Sharman were at the peak of their careers. Ed Macauley had just been traded to St. Louis, but Bill Russell was about to take his place. With that kind of talent on the premises, even a Heinsohn could get lost in the shuffle.

Which is exactly what happened to him. He once led both teams in scoring in a Celtics victory over the Minneapolis Lakers at Seattle, and earned only a single line of newspaper type for his trouble. Seattle fans, who don't get much chance to see big league basketball, flocked out to watch Russell, Cousy and Sharman, as well as Elgin Baylor of the Lakers. Before the game, all four were busy signing autographs, while everyone else on the two teams, including Heinsohn, was ignored.

The morning after the game, Heinsohn had breakfast with Gene Conley. As the two sat unnoticed in the hotel coffee shop, Conley opened the paper to the sports page to read the account of the game.

"Anything interesting?" asked Heinsohn.

"Just the usual," Conley replied. "The guy writes all about Russell's rebounding, Cousy's ball handling, Sharman's shooting and Baylor's all-round play. Oh yes—and you're mentioned right at the end."

"What does it say?" Heinsohn asked.

" 'Heinsohn scored 38 points,' " Conley read.

"That," Tommy remarked, "is the story of my life."

Heinsohn's teammates resented his treatment at the hands of press and public more than Tommy did himself. "One of my pet peeves," said Sharman, "is that Heinsohn doesn't get more recognition. He's as good as Baylor, but the only people who seem to know it are the basketball players."

Cousy agreed. "Heinsohn can do everything Baylor can do," he said one day. "On top of that, he's the best offensive rebounder in the business."

Even the league was forced to overlook him several times. An N.B.A. rule sets a limit of three men from any one team to participate in the All-Star game. Heinsohn missed three in a row because Russell, Cousy and Sharman ranked ahead of him. Until 1961, when Tommy replaced the fading Sharman, the only All-Star game he had played was in 1957, when he was the league's rookie-of-the-year.

Heinsohn never really minded playing second fiddle. After the Celtics won their first championship in 1957, he said, "I'd rather be on a winner with a dozen stars than on a loser with none."

As far as the Celtics are concerned, there never has been a question about Heinsohn's status as a star. Tommy gave them muscle when he joined them after graduating from Holy Cross in 1956, and muscle was just what they needed.

Tommy Heinsohn

Until Heinsohn came along, they never had had a great rebound man. Tommy, six feet seven and 220 pounds, was a match for anyone in the league in the bruising battles under the boards.

Thanks partly to him, the Celtics, who had never won a title before, got off to their fastest start. Hardly a month after the season began, they led the Eastern Division by ten games. Then they slipped a bit, but Russell came in late December and they went on to the championship. Without the rebounds of Heinsohn and Russell, the Celtics were only a mediocre team defensively; with the two newcomers, they were the best in the league, as, in fact, they still are.

Only their most rabid followers realize that Heinsohn has led the team in scoring every year since the 1959–60 season. The Celtics are not noted for individual scoring fireworks, another factor which has rubbed some of the luster off Heinsohn's achievements. But Tommy's consistency is remarkable. He was 11th among the league's scorers in 1962, and he has never been lower than 13th. Most of the men ahead of him are centers; Heinsohn ranks with the best cornermen in the league.

Because he is still a little basket-happy, his mates call him "Gunner" and "Ack-Ack." He can shoot many different ways, but his most spectacular is a line drive throw which he can pour in from practically any angle and from as far out as 30 feet when he's on the beam. He rifles the ball off his ear like a baseball player, and he's so accurate that he usually puts it through the hoop without its touching the rim.

Heinsohn has more scoring shots than anyone else in the league, including the fabulous Wilt Chamberlain. He's big enough to tip the ball in during scrimmages under the basket, or to pour it in on a layup. He can score by driving in with both hands, and he can also hook the ball in with either hand. He has a good set shot and sometimes even collects points on one-handed set shots.

With all this equipment, Heinsohn averages almost exactly 21 points a game. But he has the most spectacular ups and downs of anyone in the N.B.A. He tries so many shots from so many angles that he has to miss a good many of them. He can be ice cold for half a game, then suddenly get red hot.

"The worst nightmares I have," said a rival coach, "are dreams about Heinsohn with a hot hand. He can absolutely kill you."

In the 1957 All-Star game, Tommy took 17 shots in 23 minutes while scoring 5 baskets. Andy Phillip later remarked, "That's more than I took in all my All-Star games combined." In the ten playoff games the Celtics had that year, Heinsohn shot 90 baskets in 231 tries. Only Bob Pettit, the St. Louis Hawks' center, took more shots and scored more points.

Tommy was the star of the pressure-packed final playoff game, which went into two overtime periods before the Celtics won it. Heinsohn poured in 37 points that day, and he was so exhausted when he was taken out that he left the game in tears.

Tense and emotional on the court, Heinsohn is a different man off it. Relaxed and good-natured, he goes around with a perpetual grin on his handsome face. He's the club comedian, a ribber, a perpetrator of practical jokes.

His sense of humor buoyed him up on what he still describes as the "worst day of my life." Heinsohn sells life insurance, and the day started with an early-morning telephone call canceling a $150,000 policy. He drove to his office in downtown Worcester, Massachusetts, where he lives, and found a parking tag on his car when he came out. He got stopped for speeding on the road to Boston, then was late for Celtics' practice and had to pay a fine. While the team was working out, a sneak thief broke into the locker room and, among other things, stole Heinsohn's wallet with $150 in it.

As he got ready to leave for home, Tommy told his troubles to Red Auerbach. The coach, a prime practical joker himself, was so sympathetic that he gave Heinsohn a cigar which Tommy lit just before starting his car for the drive home. It exploded. So did Tommy. The ridiculous denouement to the dreary day tickled him so much he couldn't drive for fifteen minutes.

He once startled everyone at a costume party by going dressed as Little Lord Fauntleroy, encasing his huge frame in rompers and his head in a bonnet with a long ribbon trailing from it, and carrying a lollipop. He's a magnificent mimic, and can effectively imitate almost everyone he knows.

While it happens rarely, there are times when he can provide a little comic relief in the heat of a basketball game. Once knocked flat by an opponent's elbow, he had to be brought around by the Celtics' trainer.

"How do you feel?" the trainer asked when Heinsohn regained his wind.

Without moving from his position flat on his back on the floor, Heinsohn replied, "Well, I'll *try* to continue." With that he jumped up and scored five quick baskets.

Once, with the Celtics far ahead of the Knickerbockers at Madison Square Garden, he leaped up for the ball, missed, grabbed the basket and started swinging on it. The Celtics spent the rest of the evening shooting at a bent rim, and Heinsohn spent the rest of the week explaining his bizarre performance to an angry league president. The N.B.A. then put in a rule prohibiting basket-swinging.

Heinsohn is amazingly versatile. He amuses himself and his teammates by drawing caricatures and cartoons. He spends many hours in the attic of his Worcester home, which his wife fixed up as a studio for him. The house is full of his oil paintings, some of them unusually good.

He ran a sports show on a local radio station for four years, but had to give it up because of business pressure. As an agent for the Worcester State Mutual, Heinsohn sells nearly a million dollars of life insurance a year, even though he can devote full attention to it only during the basketball off-season. Among other things, he is also the player representative of the Celtics, and was one of the planners for the pension program installed by the league in 1961.

Heinsohn, born in Newark and brought up in Union City, New Jersey, started playing basketball in the sixth grade. At St. Michael's High School, he was so outstanding that he made the All-American schoolboy team in his junior year. His high school sweetheart, Diane Regenhard, was as crazy about basketball as he. She captained the St. Michael's girls team and played in a national tournament at Kansas City.

Scouts from nearly fifty colleges, promising everything from tuition to the moon, camped at Tommy's doorstep his senior year. He had ideas about taking pre-medical courses, and was given encouragement at some of the colleges that wanted him. But at Holy Cross, he was told that if he took a pre-med course he'd be too busy to play basketball.

"They were the only ones who leveled with me," he said later. "That's why I went there."

As a sophomore, Heinsohn played on the same team with Togo Palazzi, then one of the outstanding college basketball players in the country. The two teamed up to give Holy Cross a glittering record of 26 victories in 28 games that year. After Palazzi left, Heinsohn carried the Crusaders to a 19–7 record in 1955 and a 22–5 mark in 1956.

In the meantime, he and Bob Cousy, another Holy Cross boy, became close friends. At Cousy's urging, Heinsohn decided to make his home in Worcester, and the two now live within a few blocks of each other. Tommy and Diane were married while he was still in college.

As outstanding in the classroom as on the basketball court, Heinsohn made the dean's list four years in a row. As a senior, he won the Varsity Club award for being the best student-athlete in college. He also made All-American that year.

The Celtics signed him on schedule, but gave him a good scare first. With the entire Holy Cross team depending on him, Heinsohn had to pace himself in college, and Auerbach was afraid he might loaf as a pro. So just before calling Tommy in to sign a contract, Auerbach announced at a sports luncheon that Heinsohn would never make it with the Celtics if he took it as easy as he had at Holy Cross.

Heinsohn, determined to show Auerbach that he could go at top speed as long as he was on the court, turned out to be one of the hardest workers on the team. The only thing Auerbach has to warn him about today is a tendency to get careless on defense, usually the result of anxiety to score.

When Russell joined the team in December of 1956, he and Heinsohn delightedly recalled their only previous meeting. They had played against each other in a Madison Square Garden tournament when Russell was at the University of San Francisco. U.S.F. won the game, but when it was over, Russell asked Heinsohn, "Man, how do you sink those 40-foot hook shots?"

There are times when he still asks. So does everyone else in the N.B.A.

11

JERRY LUCAS

JERRY LUCAS may not be the greatest basketball player of all time, as some of his supporters insist, but he's certainly one of the most remarkable personalities the game has ever produced. This six-foot, eight-inch three-time All-American star at Ohio State is almost too good to be true. He led the Buckeyes to one N.C.A.A. championship and the threshold of two others. He was twice named the player-of-the-year and once the sportsman-of-the-year. From 1960 through 1962, he was one of the highest scorers in college ranks. He could have been at the top if he elected to shoot more baskets, but he preferred to share honors with his teammates. He threw the ball to them more often than at the hoop.

A brilliant student, he went through Ohio State on an academic scholarship. He has the ideals of a boy scout, and lives up to them. He is married to a beautiful girl whom he met on the college campus. He is shy, self-effacing, and interested in the welfare of others. He can take his basket-

Jerry Lucas

Wide World Photo

ball or leave it alone, and his plans for the future call for
only a temporary professional career.

For years Lucas denied intentions of entering the pro
game at all, for he has always refused to accept the idea
that his world must begin and end on the basketball court.
When he suddenly signed in May of 1962 with the Cleveland Pipers in the struggling American Basketball League,
he set forth in a magazine article his precise reasons for
changing his mind. Lucid and logical, they were thoroughly
consistent with the pattern of his well-organized life.

It was a life that seemed tied irrevocably to basketball
right from the start. A huge baby who weighed ten pounds
and measured 21 inches at birth, Jerry was born in Middletown, Ohio, one of the most basketball-mad communities
in America. Situated between Dayton and Cincinnati, this
city of 42,000 has backboards in every yard and courts all
over the place. Several are equipped with lights so no time
will be wasted after the sun goes down.

Baby boys were given rattles for one hand and basket-
balls for the other, and Jerry was no exception. There were
formal teams even in grade school. Jerry played for the
fourth grade team at the Sherman School, which lost once
near the end of its season. It was the last losing game Jerry
played for eight years. His teams won every one they played
until his senior year in high school. Even then, Middletown
was undefeated until the semifinals of the state schoolboy
championships, when it lost to North Columbus High
School.

The winning habit was so ingrained in Lucas that he
found it hard to imagine losing. Ohio dropped only seven
games throughout Jerry's career as a varsity player. The
losses hardly seemed to bother him, a circumstance that

worried some Buckeye fans, and even his close friends often found hard to understand.

"I play a defeat over and over," said John Havlicek, Lucas's former roommate and co-star at Ohio. "With Luke, it's as if it never happened."

In explanation of this equanimity in the face of basketball disaster, Lucas once said, "We have won so much that I always think we are going to win until the game is actually over. Then it's too late to think about, so I don't. You should worry about the problems of the future, not the past."

His coach, Fred Taylor, with a fine understanding of his star's thinking, never tried to change it.

"He has tremendous pride," Taylor said. "Nobody works harder. When the chips are down, he's fantastic. What more can I ask of him?"

Whatever question there may ever have been about Lucas's attitude, there was none about the quality of his performance. He was the inspiration, as well as the top scorer, rebounder and passer of his team. He was named the Most Valuable Player of the N.C.A.A. tournament two years in a row, and missed out the third year only because he played with bad knees, which kept him from being at the top of his game. With him, Ohio was a constant threat; without him, it was just another good college team.

All by himself, Lucas led the Buckeyes to the 1960 national championships, as they defeated California in the N.C.A.A. finals. Thanks to Jerry, they won 32 straight games in 1961 and came within a single point of whipping Cincinnati in overtime a year later. In 1962, they lost to Cincinnati again, but Jerry was not a factor in the finals.

For a man who didn't seem to care whether he won or

lost, Lucas gave himself completely to basketball once a game began. He floated up and down the court like a will-o'-the-wisp, moving effortlessly and gracefully, and always managing to be in the right place at the right time. His knees, weakened from years of play on cement courts in Middletown, often gave him trouble in college, but he never let this keep him out of action.

Yet, he has never let himself be influenced by the game which has been so much of his life for so long. As an eighteen-year-old high school senior, he showed maturity and balance that would have done credit to a man three times his age. President of his class, an honor student and a remarkable basketball player, he was romanced by representatives of no less than 150 colleges from New England to Hawaii.

During that period, Lucas received unbelievable offers, some of which would have benefited not only himself but other members of his family. It took a level head, a stout heart and strict adherence to principle to turn them down.

One college was so eager to get him that besides giving him a full scholarship, including board, room, tuition, books and extras for four years, it was also willing to: guarantee his father, who made $6500 a year as a press man, a $15,000-a-year job; pay off the mortgage on the family home; give a scholarship to Jerry's younger brother Roy when he was ready for college; and provide Jerry with a new car and liberal expense account. Another college, on hearing about this bid, offered him the same terms plus a fully furnished house for himself after he got married.

Lucas not only turned everything down, but after a while refused even to talk to college emissaries. One of the most famous coaches in the country hung around Middletown for three days trying to see him. Finally, at the urging of his own high school coach, Jerry agreed to give the visitor the time it took to go from one class to another, less than two minutes. The coach made his offer as they walked along the corridor. Jerry politely rejected it, and proceeded to his class.

Another coach, after waiting around for nearly a week, finally managed an appointment with Jerry and his father at their home. Players all over the country had been flocking to this coach for years. Jerry wouldn't even accept an invitation to visit his campus.

The coach turned to Mark Lucas, Jerry's father, and said, "This is amazing. No boy, even one who didn't end up at my school, has ever refused an invitation to come and look at it at our expense."

"Sir," Mark replied, "if Jerry went to all the campuses where he's been invited, he'd be traveling for the next two years."

Jerry's decision to go to Ohio was greeted with surprise and skepticism among the scores of scouts and coaches who had been trying to get him. Ohio's heavy emphasis was on football, not basketball, and it was obvious that the Buckeyes hadn't offered him anywhere nearly as good a deal as he could have obtained elsewhere.

Two or three years later, Jerry explained why he selected Ohio. "Those college offers were driving me crazy," he said. "I could picture myself with a new car and my dad with a lot of money, and right away I could see myself getting into a lot of trouble. I didn't want to go too far away from home, and I didn't want an athletic scholarship. My primary interest in college was to get an education.

"Ohio was the only school which emphasized the courses

it had to offer," he added. "Everyone else talked nothing but basketball. I accepted Ohio on condition I could have an academic scholarship and that it would be understood I would have to earn the marks to maintain it. Then I could quit playing basketball whenever I felt like it."

In the summer of 1960, Jerry went to Rome with the United States Olympic basketball team, which won eight straight games and the Olympic title. Although Oscar Robertson and Jerry West, who both went on to stardom in the N.B.A., were on the same team, the coach, Pete Newell, later called Lucas "the greatest player I ever coached."

Jerry got married on his return to the States. His bride, Treva Geib, was a black-haired, brown-eyed Ohio State sophomore who stands five feet, ten inches in height. The couple took a four-room apartment about a mile off the campus, and from then on struggled on a limited budget. When a friend asked Lucas if he wished he had taken one of the offers he had so steadfastly rejected as a high school senior, he replied, "Absolutely not. We're getting by on our own, and that's the way I want it."

The following spring, he accepted an opportunity to tour Russia with an A.A.U. basketball team. It meant giving up college for a semester, but he felt it was worth while.

"These people are supposed to be our enemies," he said at the time. "I want to find out all I can about them."

Lucas got more out of the trip than all his teammates combined. He went out with an interpreter whenever he could, stopping to talk to people on the street, in shops, in subway stations, wherever he found them. He had no trouble making friends. His height alone attracted attention, and his boyish smile and friendly manner did the rest.

He left Russia convinced of everybody's good intentions.

"If the government would let the people alone," he said, "there wouldn't be anything to worry about. The people want to be friends, but the propaganda against us is enough to turn your stomach."

Ever since his high school days, Jerry had insisted that he would never play professional basketball, and he repeated this several times during his senior year at Ohio. "I've had it," he told a friend in the winter of 1961. "I've been going steadily for 15 years. Nobody could pay me enough to play any more."

But he knew that, as the biggest college basketball figure since Wilt Chamberlain, he'd be under tremendous pressure to turn pro. The Cincinnati Royals, who had N.B.A. territorial draft rights on him, had already announced they'd make him an offer too attractive to refuse. The Cleveland Pipers were ready to bid for him. On top of that, he was sure to receive dozens of opportunities to make money on short-term projects.

He agreed to make a tour with some of his teammates, giving 50 talks in 50 days and playing exhibitions at night. This meant dropping out of school for a quarter, but he and Treva needed money. Besides, it gave the other seniors on the team a chance to make something too; the tour would have been off without Lucas.

While the project was lucrative, he could have done as well with a fraction of the effort, as it turned out. Abe Saperstein, owner of the Harlem Globetrotters, offered him $10,000 to travel with that team for two weeks. Jerry had to refuse because of the previous commitment.

Pepper Wilson, general manager of the Royals, offered Lucas $100,000 for three years, the best contract ever tendered any rookie except Chamberlain. To Wilson's surprise, Jerry turned it down.

"It was just a lump of money," he wrote in *Sports Illustrated*, explaining why he agreed to play for Cleveland. "What's more, I wouldn't be able to finish at Ohio State in the near future. I now had two quarters to complete before getting a degree. I could not graduate until December, and the N.B.A. season starts much earlier. Nor did the Royals have any specific thoughts or suggestions about my future. I told Mr. Wilson that was not the kind of contract I was interested in."

This concern with his future was typical of Lucas's thinking ever since he had entered Ohio. Other athletes normally link their salaries to their futures. Lucas wasn't concerned with salary alone. He considered other factors, too.

George Steinbrenner, the president of the Pipers, had familiarized himself with every phase of Lucas's character before making an offer. Knowing how important it was to Jerry that he finish his studies, Steinbrenner got the American Basketball League to agree to delay the start of the season until December. Then the Cleveland owner went to Lucas with a carefully conceived plan.

According to Jerry's *Sports Illustrated* article, Steinbrenner offered a two-year contract instead of three. After two years the club would see that his way was paid through the graduate school of his choice. He wasn't expected to play more than two years. Steinbrenner offered what amounted to a portfolio of stocks and investments that virtually assured Jerry of an income for years. Some of these were with firms that were also interested in hiring Jerry on a career basis, once he stopped playing basketball.

"The present value of the investments," Lucas revealed, "is about $40,000. My salary with the Pipers will be roughly $10,000 a season. This adds up to much less than the Cincinnati offer. But to me it is much more in long-range terms."

Jerry's decision to play for Cleveland was a shock to the N.B.A. and the first big break the luckless A.B.L. had ever had. Not one team in the infant league had made money in 1962. With Lucas, the Pipers thought they could show a profit and help the other clubs try to struggle out of the red, for he would undoubtedly draw heavily wherever they played.

However, they folded soon after signing Lucas, so they released him from his contract. He is now signed to a new pact which permits him to take the 1962—63 season off. He will enter the professional game after completing his education.

Jerry still stands ready to play basketball for two more years, but, as always, he considers the game a means to an end, not an end in itself. He may change his mind about retiring, but the chances are he won't. It's almost certain that he'll quit before he has to—and while he's still ahead.

12

RED AUERBACH

W HEN ARNOLD (RED) AUERBACH first arrived in Boston to coach the Celtics in 1950, he was so blunt in his dealings with players, press and public that experts predicted he wouldn't last a season. Seven years later the Celtics won their first N.B.A. championship and Red's critics began to admit that he might have something. By 1962, after the Celtics had broken all records by winning their fourth straight league title and their sixth division championship in a row, even Auerbach's worst enemies were forced to concede that he was the greatest coach basketball had ever seen.

Walter Brown, the owner of the Celtics, knew it all the time. When relations between Auerbach and the generally hostile local press became particularly sticky a few years after Red arrived in Boston, Brown announced, "Auerbach is the worst public relations man and the best coach in the business."

He was quite right on both counts. Auerbach put his foot into it the day he assumed command of the Celtics. The team, a dead last in 1950 and in imminent danger of folding, had several popular, but ineffectual New England college heroes. Furthermore, the most popular of all, Bob Cousy, had just graduated from Holy Cross, and it was taken for granted that the Celtics would hasten to grab him too.

When asked about Cousy, Auerbach snapped, "Am I supposed to win or take care of the local yokels?"

"You're supposed to win," Brown assured him.

"Then we'll get rid of guys who can't help us and go after guys who can—regardless where they come from," said Auerbach.

Nothing more was said about Cousy, and he wasn't drafted by the Celtics. He came to them by other means, and was on the first squad that reported to Auerbach in the autumn of 1950. Auerbach, who made it apparent that he didn't think much of Cousy at the time, openly pointed out his faults, which, in Boston, was like knocking motherhood or putting the slug on Santa Claus. The press angrily jumped down Auerbach's throat, and the repercussions were felt for years.

As late as 1962, a diehard critic of Red, asked what he thought of the Celtics' coach, replied, "Well, maybe he's all right now, but don't forget, he passed up Cousy."

It was one of Auerbach's few mistakes, but he made up for it by his superb handling of Cousy. While others raved over Cousy's every move, Auerbach never let him forget his errors. Cousy, a man of great pride and a tremendously hard worker, strove for perfection, and came as close as any basketball player in history to attaining it. Auerbach's constant needling was a big factor in his development, just as it has been an important factor in the building of the amazing Celtics team.

Auerbach's shrewd knowledge of human nature has been as much responsible for the Celtics' success as his knowledge of basketball. He treats each of his men as an individual, playing on their emotions, their strengths and their weaknesses as a maestro plays on the strings of a violin. He knows when to criticize, when to praise, when to laugh, when to be serious, when to meddle, when to leave alone.

There is no coach with a better instinct for substituting, a most important adjunct to the pro game. Auerbach can almost sense the moment a player should come out, and he has the happy faculty of replacing him with exactly the right man.

"Which," a rival remarked, not long ago, "is easy. Look at the bench he has!"

This is true enough, of course, but the Celtics' bench is Auerbach's own. He carefully hand-picked each man, often seeing possibilities that others missed. Nobody but Auerbach wanted Sam Jones, now a starter, but originally Bill Sharman's replacement. Nobody but Auerbach wanted Satch Sanders, a backcourt man who now would be welcome on any team in the league. Nobody but Auerbach wanted Gene Conley, who filled in for Bill Russell for several years and was one of the few men, other than Russell himself, who could handle Wilt Chamberlain. Nobody but Auerbach wanted to take a chance on K.C. Jones, whose basketball skill apparently had been blunted by two years in the army.

The whole team is Auerbach's, for he is scout and general manager as well as coach of the Celtics. He buys and sells, makes deals, drafts and decides whom to keep and whom to drop. During his years in Boston, he has taken some dangerous chances, and most of them have paid off handsomely.

Red Auerbach and admirers

The most daring and sensationally successful was the
Bill Russell gamble. When Russell graduated from the University of San Francisco in 1956, there was great doubt
about his availability to any club in the N.B.A. As a member of the U.S. Olympic team, he wouldn't even turn pro
until nearly mid-season. When he did, it appeared to be a

foregone conclusion that he would sign with the Harlem Globetrotters, who had made him a fabulous offer.

But he was exactly the man Auerbach had been seeking for years. The Celtics had failed to win any titles for lack of a big man who could grab rebounds, and this was the best of Russell's many skills. Red decided it was worth making sacrifices just for the chance to dicker with the six-foot, nine-inch youth.

St. Louis had first crack at Russell, but Ben Kerner, the Hawks' owner, had little hope of getting him. Auerbach made him an offer so attractive that he couldn't turn it down. In return for draft rights to Russell, the Celtics were willing to give the Hawks Ed Macauley, an established star and a St. Louis home town favorite, and Cliff Hagan, one of the most promising rookies in the league.

If Auerbach had failed to get Russell, it could very likely have cost him his job. Red didn't even consider that possibility. He began working on Russell through mutual friends, and by the time Russell returned from the Olympic Games he had given up the idea of joining the Globetrotters and was ready to sign with the Celtics. Auerbach's daring deal provided the key to a perennial championship team.

One of Auerbach's greatest assets is his tremendous circle of friends among college coaches and former basketball players. With no farm system, the Celtics depend heavily on personal contact in their quest for new blood. Throughout the college season, Red is in constant touch with basketball men around the country. Sometimes he calls to ask about a specific player; sometimes a friend will call attention to a promising prospect.

Red is as shrewd in the conference room as on the basketball court. He is not a lawyer, but he could have been a good one. He's a master at finding legitimate loopholes in the rules and quickly taking advantage of them. He got Frank Ramsey, Cliff Hagan and Lou Tsioropoulos, stars of Kentucky's onetime "dream team," on a complicated technicality that caught the other owners flat-footed. Ramsey is still one of his stars and Hagan has been a mainstay of the Hawks ever since going to St. Louis in the Russell deal.

At court-side, Red is the great prototype of pro coaches —tough, hot-headed, argumentative and fast-thinking. For a long time, he was the most fined man in the N.B.A. He and Maurice Podoloff, its president, have carried on a running feud for years. Red takes everlasting delight in needling the roly-poly N.B.A. executive. To this day he annoys Podoloff by refusing to sign reports, in defiance of a league rule. Years ago he told Podoloff, "I can't read your letters to me. Why should I sign mine to you?"

Referees respect him because of his thorough knowledge of the rules, but they once hated to work Celtics' games. The combination of age and success has calmed Auerbach down considerably, but he used to be in the officials' hair constantly. Many of the decisions made in basketball are based on judgment, and Red's rarely agreed with that of the referees. In the early days of his coaching career, Auerbach was a nagging protester, on his feet howling at the injustice of officials from start to finish of every ball game.

A consummate actor, Red always put on a great show for the crowd. He made faces, stamped his feet, tore at his thinning hair, waved his arms, put his hands on his hips in disgust and appealed for justice to the customers, who usually responded with a chorus of boos which shook the rafters.

He has protested the height of the basket, claiming that it was lower than the regulation ten feet, and once, with a tape measure in his hand, he climbed a ladder to check. (It was within a fraction of an inch of the proper height.) Another time, he threw a punch at Kerner in an argument over the basket's height in St. Louis.

He has been escorted out of arenas by police, chased out by crowds and hounded out by angry partisan fans. He has been insulted, cursed at, swung at, laughed at, howled at and even spat at. Although he is small in stature, he isn't afraid of anyone, and has been in fights with bigger, stronger and tougher men—but no angrier.

His bluntness often got him into trouble, but this never bothered him. If he thought he was right, he said so in plain, unadorned English. Even when he knew it would cost him money in fines, he stuck by his guns. He once raised a terrible fuss over a referee's decision that cost the Celtics a game in the last second. When asked later if he was sorry, he replied, "Of course not. My remarks were strong, but not abusive. I said the call was stupid, and it was."

His diet during the basketball season is enough to give his friends the heebie-jeebies. Auerbach is a teetotaler, but he drinks chocolate milkshakes by the gallon, and at all hours of the night. He has never eaten an egg nor drunk a cup of coffee. He would rather have bad Chinese food at a hole-in-the-wall than a good steak at a fine restaurant. He has no set meal times; he eats when he feels like it. But he starves himself for hours before games, because he claims it keeps him sharp and alert.

"If you're full," he says, "you're too contented, and contented guys don't win ball games."

As every Celtics fan knows, Red is a cigar smoker, for he makes a ritual out of lighting his victory cigar. When the Celtics play at home, the fans know he figures the game is on ice when he ostentatiously pulls a stogie out of his pocket, shoves it into his mouth and puts a match to it. This happens only in the late stages of a game and when the Celtics are well ahead, and it is always greeted with a roar from the crowd.

Never an outstanding basketball player himself, Auerbach jumped into coaching with astonishingly little training. Born and brought up in Brooklyn, he went to George Washington University, where he was a fairly good little man on a mediocre team. But basketball intrigued him so much that he studied every phase of it and, while still in college, made up his mind that he wanted to coach. For this reason alone, he took a master's degree in education, then, with World War II in progress, he went into the navy under the Gene Tunney physical fitness program.

Although only in his mid-twenties, Red coached navy basketball teams, rarely playing himself. He studied and experimented, worked with players, some of whom were older than he, and learned as much about the game as he could. When the war ended, he went back to Washington, D.C., where he brashly offered his services as a coach to Mike Uline, owner of the Uline Arena in Washington. The pro league was just being formed, and Uline had the Washington Capitols' franchise.

Through his navy and college contacts, Red collected a team which he took to two Division titles in three years. The 1947 Capitols led the Eastern Division by 14 games, and once had a 17-game winning streak which still stands as a record. It was matched only by one of Auerbach's Celtics teams.

When his third season at Washington was over, Red decided to try college coaching, and he spent a few months at North Carolina. Except for this brief period, he has been in the N.B.A. steadily since the league was formed. His college career ended almost as soon as it began, for the pro game was in Auerbach's blood and he couldn't resist an offer to coach at Tri-Cities in Iowa during the 1949–50 season.

The league was then in the process of a painful transitional period. Tri-Cities was one of 17 teams, many of which were later dropped. Auerbach wasn't especially happy there, partly because the Middle West was too far from his wife and children in Washington and partly because he didn't know how long the Tri-Cities franchise would last.

It wasn't the only team in trouble that year. The Celtics had finished last, and the Boston Garden Corporation, which owned them, was ready to throw in the towel. Walter Brown, the Garden general manager, wanted to buy the team, and went to Lou Pieri, a Providence promoter, for financial help.

"I'll go in with you," Pieri said, "if you'll get Red Auerbach. That young fellow is the best basketball coach in the league."

It was the beginning of a friendship which has lasted to this day. Brown and Auerbach have never had a written contract. Every year they seal whatever salary agreement they make with a handshake. In the early years, when Brown was struggling to keep the Celtics' franchise alive, Red settled for comparatively modest salaries. After the Celtics began winning and drawing customers, the figure went up, and today Auerbach collects about $30,000 a year for his services.

In return, he has given Brown the finest aggregation of basketball players ever gathered together. A baseball fan and a great admirer of the Yankees, Red likes to think that his Celtics are the Yankees of basketball. They have the same confidence, the same *esprit de corps* and the same pride. They're the best team in the league, and Red never lets any of them forget it.

While Red has a sharp sense of humor and permits himself to relax with his players, he's a strict disciplinarian who demands absolute obedience to his rules. These are almost ridiculously simple. The men are expected to be on time to practice, to work hard and faithfully and to hustle every minute they're on the basketball floor. Auerbach doesn't care what they do off the court, and makes no attempt to police them. He concerns himself only with their activities while in uniform.

His men swear by him. A pat on the back from Red means more to them than the cheers of every fan in a sold-out arena. They work and play and battle for his approval, and he, in turn, fights for them individually and as a team.

"Other coaches may know as much basketball as Red," Frank Ramsey said not long ago, "but nobody can touch him as a handler of men."

To the world in general, Red Auerbach puts on a dour exterior, but those who can get behind it find a fun-loving character whose second favorite occupation after coaching is carrying out practical jokes. He is as often the victim as the perpetrator, which never lessens his enjoyment.

Author of a popular book of instruction called *Basketball for the Player, the Fan and the Coach,* Auerbach is one of the sports world's smartest characters. Rival coaches have been trying to get the best of him for years.

It's likely to be a long time before any of them catch up with him.

13

BOB PETTIT

Most great basketball players were stars almost from childhood, but not Bob Pettit. Now one of the smoothest athletes in the game, Pettit was such a clumsy youngster that he couldn't make his high school team until his junior year. Anyone who has ever watched him covering the length of a basketball court with the grace of a greyhound finds it hard to believe that he spent most of his adolescent years tripping over his own feet.

Pettit, clean-living and serious-minded, owes to nobody but himself the fact that he is a magnificent athlete today. He had some help along the way, but only his own perseverance and patience were responsible for his amazing transformation from an awkward incompetent to a model of basketball efficiency.

He has been the key man of the St. Louis Hawks since 1954, when he went into the N.B.A. after graduating from Louisiana State University. He was the first rookie to make the All-League team, and hasn't been off it since. He is the only man to have won the Most Valuable Player trophy for the All-Star game four different times. He has led the league in scoring and in rebounds, and has never been worse than fourth in either department of the game. His name is among the five top scorers of all time, and it's likely to remain there for some years to come.

Pettit led the Hawks to their only world's championship in 1958, after taking them to within a whisker of the title the Celtics won the previous year. The team, now a popular fixture in St. Louis, couldn't have survived without him. To this day, owner Ben Kerner says Pettit was the man who saved the franchise.

Every player in the league respects Pettit as a man and as a basketball player. They won't even allow his own boss to rob him of credit, as was graphically demonstrated after the Hawks beat the Boston Celtics in the game that clinched the title in 1958. Slater Martin was one of the Hawks' stars that night, but only as a member of the supporting cast to Pettit, for Bob scored 50 points. But Kerner, carried away by Martin's great defensive performance, exuberantly proclaimed after the game that "Martin won the championship for us."

When Bob Cousy heard about it, the Celtics' star snapped, "If he thinks anyone but Pettit won that championship, he's out of his mind."

While Pettit has had occasional better nights—he has scored over 50 points several times and once had 57 against the Detroit Pistons—he still considers that final playoff contest of the 1958 season the high spot of his career. It was played before a packed house in St. Louis with the Hawks in a three-to-two lead in games. But the Celtics were leading at the end of three periods, and the odds were heavy that they would hang on to the finish. This would

Bob Pettit

send the series back to Boston where the Celtics were almost unbeatable.

The Hawks went nowhere for half the fourth period, then suddenly Pettit caught fire. He was all over the court, stealing the ball, grabbing rebounds, tying up the opposition and, almost incidentally, pouring one shot after another through the hoop. As he converted basket after basket, the Hawks crept up until they were only a point behind with seconds to go. Pettit, his lean, graceful figure dominating the play, as it had for nearly ten minutes, made a last grab for the ball, brought it down-court and flipped it home for the score that meant the title.

It was the most spectacular one-man exhibition of short-term scoring ever seen in a playoff series. Pettit shot eight field goals in the last part of the final period, and scored 19 of the Hawks' 21 points during that time. It gave him a game total of 19 field goals for 38 points from the floor. He also sank 12 out of 15 foul shots.

His performance against the same Celtics in the playoffs the year before was almost as spectacular, but Pettit discounts it entirely because the Hawks lost the series. It certainly wasn't his fault. He had 37 points in the first game, which the Hawks won. He shot the winning basket for St. Louis in the third game, in which he totaled 26 points. In the next four games, he scored 33 in the first, 33 in the second, 32 in the third and 39 in the pressure-packed double overtime finale.

Just as the last buzzer of that game sounded, Pettit tried to tip in a rebound from a bad angle. Nobody knows how he even got close since he was on the far side of the court when the play began. He touched the ball with his fingers, and it teetered on the rim for an instant, but then fell outside.

When an observer congratulated him later for his remarkable play throughout the series, he looked up and said, "I should have had that last basket. It was my fault we lost." Not a single person in the Boston Garden that day agreed with him.

In the days before Wilt Chamberlain came along to make a shambles of the record books, Pettit was one of the game's most consistent scoring leaders. He nearly won the title in his rookie year, for he led the N.B.A. until the last few weeks of the 1954–55 season. Then he tired, but his total of 1466 was the highest made by a rookie up to that time.

He went home to Baton Rouge, Louisiana, and spent the summer putting on weight and building up his muscles. He reported back to the Hawks ten pounds heavier, and proceeded to lead the league in scoring.

"My trouble last year," he said at the time, "was that my strength hadn't caught up to my height, and I ran out of steam."

He has rarely run out of steam since, another tribute to his own determination. "You learn something new every year," he once said. "It's up to you to make the most of it."

He learned another lesson when he broke his wrist in February of 1957 in a game against the Celtics. "It was the first time I was ever hurt," he said later. "It taught me that any game might be your last, so the game you're playing right now is the most important one of your life."

The wrist fracture failed to stop him. He played the rest of the season with a cast on his forearm. By acting as if each game would be his last, he literally pulled the Hawks into the playoffs.

They had three coaches in three weeks that year. Red Holzman started the season, followed by Slater Martin, who quit in favor of Alex Hannum. By the time Hannum took over, everyone on the team except Pettit had ideas on how the club should be run.

"The Hawks started the season with one coach and ten players," one St. Louis writer said. "Before they were through, they had nine coaches and one player. While everyone else did the suggesting, Pettit went out and scored the points."

Bob's All-Star performances have been among the best of his career. He has scored more points in this East-West classic than any other player, and he holds several scoring records. In 1962, after setting a mark of 27 rebounds and leading the West to a 150–130 victory, he was voted the Most Valuable Player, but this was an old story for Pettit. He first won the honor in 1956, did it again in 1958, then shared it with Elgin Baylor of the Lakers in 1959.

Since there had never before been a tie, the league had only one trophy ready to present the winner. As Pettit shook hands with Baylor, he said to the rookie, "You keep it. I already have a couple." So Baylor took the prize home with him, while Pettit waited for a duplicate trophy.

Actually, he missed out on the award on one of his best nights. In the 1961 game he set a record of 19 points for one half and a record total of 29 for the game, but he lost the M.V.P. trophy by a single vote to Oscar Robertson of Cincinnati.

While Pettit has all the tools needed by a top-flight professional basketball player, his best shot is a fabulous jumper, on which he scores about half his points. Pettit has remarkable spring in his legs and this, combined with his great height, puts him head and shoulders over most of the other men in the league when he's in range of the basket. He has tremendous endurance, built up by long years of working with weights during the off-season. A physical culture enthusiast, he is always in such splendid shape that he can play all but a few minutes of every game.

All of which is a far cry from the almost anemic stringbean that Bob was as a kid in Baton Rouge. The only child of wealthy parents, he might have grown up a spoiled brat if he weren't so level-headed. His father, who once was sheriff of Baton Rouge, owns a successful insurance and real estate firm and has other business interests. Bob had everything he wanted as a child. He never had a day of financial worry in his life.

This stood him in good stead when he first talked terms with Kerner after graduating from Louisiana State University in 1954. The Hawks were then in Milwaukee, and struggling. Kerner offered Pettit a good contract, but Bob calmly demanded five thousand dollars more.

"Later," Kerner said. "Right now I can't afford to give it to you."

"I guess I'll go home then," Pettit said. "It doesn't make any difference to me whether I play basketball or go into business."

Kerner hastily changed his mind, and gave Bob what he wanted. The relationship between the two has since been one of close friendship and mutual respect, and Kerner now pays his star somewhere in the neighborhood of $30,000 a year.

Pettit comes by his height honestly. His father, Robert Pettit, Sr., stands six feet, four inches. He played football and baseball at Westminster College in Denver. Bob's mother is not unusually tall, but she had four brothers ranging in height between six feet, two and six, five.

Bob grew up a mile from the L.S.U. campus. He was interested in all sports, but not very good at any of them.

As a freshman at Baton Rouge High School, he stood five, ten and weighed 118 pounds, and went out for football, basketball and baseball. The first time he ever scrimmaged in football, an opposing back ran right over him and went 65 yards for a touchdown. Bob played in three freshman basketball games and failed to score a point. In the spring, when he stood nearly six feet, he decided to go out for baseball, figuring he was built for a first baseman. He was the first boy cut from the squad.

The next year Bob passed up football, but reported for varsity basketball. The coach ran out of uniforms before reaching him, and that seemed to be the end of his schoolboy sports career. The disappointed youngster suffered further embarrassment when he even failed to do well in a Baton Rouge church league, made up mostly of boys who, like himself, couldn't make the high school team.

Bob's father, who had gone through much the same frustration in his own youth, put up a basket in the back yard. After that, the boy spent every spare minute practicing. Day after day, week after week, month after month, he shot at the back-yard basket, sometimes with friends, more often alone. After a while, he developed an awkward, but fairly accurate push shot.

More important, he was growing. By his junior year in high school, he stood six, five, and was the tallest boy in school. This time, the coach made sure he had a uniform, and Bob found himself on a formal basketball team for the first time in his life. The coach tried to help him, but there wasn't much anyone could do for him. Bob was still growing, and only practice and more practice would ever cure his clumsiness.

He did better as a six-foot, seven-inch senior, and before

the season was over, began to look more like a basketball player. Baton Rouge, with Pettit scoring most of the points, won the Louisiana State title that year. Bob averaged over 31 points a game, although he still insists that his height alone enabled him to do it.

"I was the biggest schoolboy in the state," he says. "All I had to do was stand in front of the basket with my arms stretched out and shoot. Nobody else could reach the ball."

While a few other colleges made attempts to get him, nobody but L.S.U. had a chance. Having grown up in the shadow of the university, Pettit didn't even consider the idea of going elsewhere. And, now nearly at his full growth of six, nine, he reported hopefully to the freshman coach, John Chaney.

But Bob was still little more than a big awkward kid. He couldn't drive, fake, pass off the pivot or play defense. He was beginning to develop his jump shot, but he didn't even know how to set up a layup. Everyone took it for granted that he would play center. With his height, it seemed ridiculous to put him anywhere else.

Chaney worked on him, and Bob was showing progress by the end of his freshman year. Even then, however, there was no question in his mind that he would have to make his own improvements.

"They could teach me how something should be done," he recalled later, "but they couldn't do the coordinating for me. I had to learn that for myself."

He got help from an unexpected source the summer after his freshman year, when he worked as a camp counselor in Wisconsin. There he met Ray Meyer, who had coached George Mikan at De Paul. Meyer took a liking to the big youth, who reminded him of Mikan, and worked with Pettit all summer. Bob studied movies of the great Minneapolis star, with Meyer at his elbow pointing out the virtues and flaws.

Bob came home a better basketball player and proved it during his sophomore year when he averaged 25 points a game for L.S.U. He did better than that as a junior, and by his senior year he made All-American.

Before accepting Kerner's invitation to go to Milwaukee, Bob had several talks with Frank Brian, a distant cousin, who played for Fort Wayne.

"There are other things I could do," Bob said, "but the idea of playing professionally interests me. What do you think?"

"I'd play if I were you," Brian replied. "You've got the build and the ability. I've enjoyed it, and I think you will too. I can't think of a more pleasant way to make a living."

Brian probably lived to regret his advice, for he had to play against Pettit for the next two years before he retired from the game.

Pettit didn't exactly burn up the N.B.A. in the first few weeks of his pro career. As a college center, he had been king of all he surveyed. Always the tallest man on the floor, he didn't find it too difficult to outplay every center he faced. But it was a different story in the pro league. Every center in the N.B.A. except Ed Macauley was either taller or more rugged than Pettit, and even Macauley gave him a rough time at the backboards.

Holzman solved the problem by switching Bob to a forward where he had more leeway to move up and down the court, and where he wouldn't be the target of every other big man in the league. From then on, Pettit was a standout.

During the years since, Pettit has found a unique place for himself in the N.B.A. He is one of the quietest men in the league, rarely saying much either on or off the court. Unlike most players, Bob never openly objects to a referee's decision. If he has anything to say to an official about a call he doesn't like, he says it later in an aside during a time out or between periods.

Although Pettit spent one year in Milwaukee and has played in St. Louis since 1955, he never thought of leaving Baton Rouge permanently. One of the most eligible bachelors in the sports world, Bob can't get home fast enough after the basketball season ends. He takes a short vacation, then puts in regular office hours until the next basketball season comes around.

He helps his father in the family business, and supplements it with insurance and real estate interests of his own. Almost all his spare cash goes into Baton Rouge property, which he handles with the same skill that he handles a basketball. As a result, Pettit today is one of the wealthiest athletes in the country.

His ambition is to play on another championship team, but he knows there is less and less chance. Although he still keeps himself in magnificent physical condition, he turned thirty in 1962, and he realizes that he can't last forever. Aside from that, the great Hawks teams of the late 1950's have been replaced by a somewhat tired, disorganized ball club which was torn by dissension during the 1961–62 season.

As always, Bob minded his own business and kept out of the arguments that blasted the team apart. He just continued to play his usual brilliant game. If his teammates had followed his example, things might have gone better for the club. Perhaps, with Pettit as the stabilizer, it can yet regain its place in the basketball sun.

Oscar Robertson

14

OSCAR ROBERTSON

When Oscar Robertson, the "Big O," starts driving down a basketball court, he looks like a big, sleek, graceful cat. In Cincinnati, where he has given the Royals stature they never had before, he delights the thousands of new friends he has made for the team with the smooth execution of his remarkable play. After Maurice Stokes suffered his paralyzing illness, the only star the Royals had was Jack Twyman, and he couldn't carry the team all by himself. In common with everyone else connected with the club, Twyman waited impatiently for Robertson to graduate from the University of Cincinnati and become eligible for the pro game.

This happened in 1960. Ever since, Robertson has been one of the shining stars of the N.B.A. The first thing he did was assume the crown long worn by Bob Cousy as the best play-maker in the league. The Big O topped everyone in assists both in 1961 and 1962. He was also third in scoring both years, averaging nearly 31 points per game each season.

His accuracy, always great in college when he was a three-time All-American, three-time scoring champion and three-time player-of-the-year, was fully as deadly in the faster company of the pros. In 1961, he was fourth in field goal percentages, with a mark of .472. The next year, he and Twyman were tied for third at .478.

Robertson was not only rookie-of-the-year, but he became only the second rookie to win most valuable player honors in the All-Star game. In the 153–131 victory by the West team over the East in 1961, Oscar led both teams in assists and was the West's second highest scorer behind Bob Pettit of the Hawks. Both that year and the next, he made the All-League first team.

Beyond everything else, Robertson is enjoying himself for perhaps the first time in his life. The Big O is far better adjusted to his problems than he ever was in college. While he was courteous to outsiders during his undergraduate years, he was truly happy only on the basketball court. Off it, he was frequently moody, unhappy and resentful, for, as a proud and sensitive man, he found it hard to accept the slights to which he was exposed because of his race.

Cincinnati is a northern city geographically, but it has some of the characteristics of the South in its handling of Negroes, and Robertson, whose home was Indianapolis, was quick to take offense at insults that came his way. Even in his senior year, when as the best-known national sports figure in the history of the university, he was a campus hero, he never felt at ease among his fellow students.

"I got this far," he said one day. "Now all I want to do is get it over with. In June it'll be finished. I can hardly wait."

Twice during the three years that he traveled about the country with the basketball team, he suffered humiliation so intense that he nearly left school. The first time came in his sophomore year when he wasn't permitted to stay with his teammates at the plush Shamrock Hotel in Houston.

Later he told a friend, "If that happens again, I'll take the first bus to Indianapolis."

The university didn't let it happen again. After that, the team arranged to stay in dormitories or fraternity houses when it played in the South.

A year after the Houston affair, Robertson's ears burned with the insults of ill-mannered fans at the Dixie Classic in Raleigh, North Carolina. That time he actually did leave school for a few days, but wiser, cooler friends persuaded him to return. Once again, the university made sure there would be no repetition. In Robertson's senior year, the team went to Madison Square Garden to play in New York's Holiday Festival instead of returning to Raleigh.

All of this didn't seem to affect the Big O's play. Mad or glad, happy or unhappy, slighted or lionized, he starred whenever he stepped out on the basketball floor. The game seemed to have almost a tranquilizing effect on this troubled youth who took the pressures of basketball in stride.

He was on the spot in more ways than one. On the day before Robertson reported for varsity basketball as a sophomore at Cincinnati, George Smith, the athletic director, called a special meeting of the team and told the boys, "You were a good team before, but with Robertson you're going to be a better one—maybe a great one. He'll get all the publicity and all the headlines. But if you play with him, you'll go farther than you've ever gone before."

The men on the ball club cooperated, and the Bearcats

indeed went farther than they ever had before. They won three straight Missouri Valley championships, and had a three-year record of 89 victories against only 9 defeats. But the one thing Oscar wanted most, an N.C.A.A. title, was denied him. Cincinnati reached the semifinals two years out of the three that he played there, but got no further.

While Robertson himself never enjoyed the thrill of playing on a championship team, he left his alma mater an unusual legacy. Paul Hogue, Tony Yates and Tom Thacker, all outstanding young Negro players, went to the University of Cincinnati solely because of their admiration for the Big O. They sparked the Bearcats to the N.C.A.A. titles in 1961 and 1962, as Cincinnati became only the fourth team in the tournament's history to win back-to-back championships.

From his perch among the pros, Robertson got a vicarious thrill out of those titles. Actually, he was prouder of his college as an alumnus than he ever had been as a student. To some of the same friends to whom he had complained, he recently said, "I hope they never get beaten."

The Royals, who moved from Rochester to Cincinnati at the end of the 1957 season, suffered through three losing years waiting for the Big O to complete his college career. They had to bid against the Harlem Globetrotters in order to get him, and succeeded with a three-year $100,000 contract.

Robertson might have signed for less, since the Globetrotters, with their clowning and their constant traveling, hardly appealed to him. Besides, he found the Royals more of a challenge. He was eager to see how well he could do in competition with the world's greatest basketball players.

He wasted no time proving that he belonged, and while the Royals didn't get very far because they needed more than even the Big O could give them, they pulled in the customers as they never had before. Every basketball fan in Cincinnati wanted to see Robertson in a Royals uniform, and nobody cared whether the team won or lost.

The club attracted more fans in the first quarter of the 1960–61 season than it had during the entire year before. The Big O was solely responsible for this amazing turnout. And, if there was any doubt about that, it was quickly dispelled when he got hurt in January. The Cincinnati Gardens looked like a wilderness in the two home games which Robertson missed.

Altogether, he was out four games that time and the Royals lost them all. Robertson's return marked the end of the slump. The Big O had one of his best nights, scoring 32 points from the pivot, and leading the Royals to their first victory over the Celtics in Cincinnati since 1958. Not only that, but almost a full house was on hand to see him.

At a shade under six feet, five, Robertson is the N.B.A.'s shortest center, when he plays there, which is most of the time. It doesn't really matter, however, for he can outjump almost everyone else in the business, and has the strength to battle for the ball at the backboards. When he leaps, his outstretched hands are ten inches above the rim of the basket.

The Big O doesn't look big, compared to other basketball stars. He weighs only 195, but every ounce of it is solid muscle. He keeps himself in perfect shape, and is a dedicated student of the game. He wants to be the perfect player, and is gradually moving toward that goal. In the comparatively short time that he's been in the N.B.A., he has learned the strengths and weaknesses of everyone else in the loop.

Oscar was born in 1938 on his grandfather's farm near

Charlotte, Tennessee. His father's grandfather, a former slave, was reported to be the oldest person in the United States when he died in 1954 at the age of 116. Close contact with this remarkable old man who could remember the pre-Civil War days might well have had much to do with the youth's acute awareness of his race.

When Oscar was four years old, his parents took him and his two older brothers to live in Indianapolis. He did not have a particularly happy childhood because his mother and father were divorced soon after leaving Tennessee, and Mrs. Robertson was too busy earning a living to spend much time at home.

A beautician by trade, Oscar's mother has considerable musical talent. She is a gospel singer, and belongs to a choral group, part of whose repertoire consists of religious music which she has composed. Oscar, who adores her, always resented her having to work. He was particularly upset while he was in college when she was forced to return to her job after recovering from an illness.

"Some day," Oscar told her, "I'll get those bills paid, and you won't have to work any more."

Oscar went to an all-Negro high school, Crispus Attucks, and it was there that he became a great basketball player. Ray Crowe, brother of George Crowe of major league baseball fame, was his coach, and recognized his potential immediately. At the boy's request, Crowe gave him a key to the school gym so Oscar could work out weekends and during vacation periods.

His grace, his remarkable reflexes and his devotion to the game impressed Crowe from the start. "If you practice faithfully and take care of yourself," the coach told Oscar when he was a freshman, "we'll have one of the best school-boy teams in this area and you can go on to become one of the great stars of the game."

Oscar did as he was told, and the first part of Crowe's prophecy came true by the time the boy was a junior. Even then, college coaches were keeping an eye on him, and they really flocked after him the next year. Oscar led Crispus Attucks to the first undefeated season ever enjoyed by an Indiana high school team, and it became the first all-Negro team to win the state championship.

An excellent student, Oscar had good enough marks to get into almost any college he wanted to, and there were representatives from 75 of them camped at his doorstep by the time he was ready to graduate. Even Adolph Rupp, who had never had a Negro player at Kentucky, offered him a scholarship, but Oscar had no desire to become a trail blazer of this nature. He accepted the University of Cincinnati partly because it was near home and partly because it had a cooperative work plan. This would enable him to make extra money as well as develop contacts which might be of future value.

But he ran into problems because of his race almost as soon as he arrived on the campus. He quickly learned that, while he might be a hero on the basketball court, off it he would have to be completely on his own. His only close friends were other Negro students, and there weren't very many of them. And while they accepted the situation, Robertson found it impossible to adjust to it.

He was the nation's leading college scorer, an All-American and the player-of-the-year in his sophomore year, yet it was a year of disillusionment for him. He was asked for his autograph but not for his time. He was pointed out but ignored. He had white teammates and admirers, but no white friends.

"It's a crazy world," he told a writer who interviewed him on the campus that year, "and I can't like it. I have no social life here."

The fact that he wouldn't go to movies because he was afraid of what it might do to his eyes didn't keep him from knowing there were certain theaters in Cincinnati where he wouldn't have been welcome anyhow. Every slight was a deep cut, and soon he was the most famous "loner" in town.

Yet he never lost his temper, nor did he lose patience with those who wanted to talk basketball with him. He was always cooperative with photographers and courteous with reporters. However, he had very little to say, and was a hard man to interview. His standard comment after a big night was, "Well, we won—and they lost."

One veteran New York writer remarked after meeting Robertson for the first time, "This guy makes Calvin Coolidge sound like a chatterbox."

Even though rival defenses were rigged against him wherever he went, Robertson continued to be one of the nation's most brilliant players all through his college career. He wasn't the first to make All-American three straight years, but he was the first to capture the nation's scoring title three times in a row, and the first to be named player-of-the-year three times.

At one time or another, he set scoring records for the N.C.A.A. tournament, the Missouri Valley Conference and the State of Ohio. When he scored 56 points against Seton Hall as a sophomore, it was a Madison Square Garden record which had never been matched by either amateurs or pros up to that time.

As the years went on, Robertson's resentment led to his losing interest in his studies, and at one point he came close to flunking out.

"What difference does it make whether I do or not?" he said to a friend. "My future is in basketball anyhow."

Even though he disapproved of the Globetrotters, and didn't relish the prospect of one-night stands all over the world, he was tempted to join them if only for the companionship. He had been happiest in an all-Negro high school, and at one point he thought this all-Negro professional team might give him the same pleasure.

But he only toyed with the idea. During his junior year, after having worked under the university's cooperative plan for the Cincinnati Gas and Electric Company, he got a job with an insurance firm run by one of the Royals' executives. From then on, he knew he would go into the pro league if the team made him a fair offer.

He didn't join the Royals immediately on becoming eligible because of the 1960 Olympics. The Big O delayed signing until his return from Rome, where he and Jerry West co-captained the undefeated United States team. Jerry Lucas was also on that club. As soon as they got home, West and Robertson turned pro.

By this time, Robertson was a changed man, thanks to a brilliant young grade school teacher whom he married after finishing college. Yvonne Robertson, who held a master's degree from Columbia, was probably the first person who had ever completely understood this moody campus hero. She gradually convinced him that life wasn't all bad, that there are broad-minded people in the world as well as bigots, and that a Negro, in common with everyone else, could expect to get out of life only as much as he was willing to put in.

Robertson, for the first time in years, felt that he belonged somewhere. The man who refused to go to movies has become a television fan. The man who thought nobody liked him has a host of friends, and not all are Negroes. Sometimes he helps his wife correct her school papers, sometimes he spends hours with her listening to good music and sometimes he takes her out to dinner. Instead of fighting the places where he knows he's not welcome, he now goes where he knows he's accepted.

"I know a lot of things are wrong," he says today, "but I'm not a crusader. I can't change the world."

His personal hero is Jackie Robinson, the man who broke big league baseball's color line.

"He did something few of us could have done," Oscar once told a friend. "He took a horrible beating for the sake of a principle, and all of us gained by it. Every Negro in America owes him a debt of gratitude. I'd give anything if I could be like him."

Since there is only one Jackie Robinson, the Big O can't be like him. But he can be a hero to his people in his own right, for he has overcome prejudices of his own fully as bad as those from which he suffered so many indignities.

He's not only a great basketball player, but a mature, well-adjusted man. Considering what he went through in college, this in itself is a triumph.

15

JERRY WEST

The Los Angeles Lakers had won the first two
games of the 1962 N.B.A. Western Division playoffs over
the Detroit Pistons, and were trying to make it three
straight. But the Pistons took an early lead in the third
game, and still held it halfway through the last quarter.

Then Jerry West, a six-three midget among the titans of
pro basketball, began acting like Bob Cousy, a habit he
assumes whenever the going gets tough. For ten minutes
there didn't seem to be anybody else on the floor as the Los
Angeles backcourt marvel took charge of the ball game. He
poured in eleven points so fast that the Pistons didn't know
what hit them. The Lakers won the game, made it three in
a row and went on to take the series and qualify for the
finals against the mighty Boston Celtics.

Thanks partly to West, they nearly pulled that one out
too. With the series even at a game apiece, the Celtics
wanted desperately to win the third contest, which was in

Los Angeles. And, with a three-point lead and only five seconds to go, they apparently had it all wrapped up.

But West was at the foul line, and he calmly sank both his shots. Before the Celtics recovered from that blow, West stole the ball from under their noses and poured in the winning basket just before the final buzzer sounded. The Celtics, who might otherwise have won an easy title, were forced to go the limit. The Lakers carried them all the way to a seventh-game overtime before they could clinch their fourth straight championship.

The man who gave Boston such a rough time was simply running true to form. Jerry West, a two-time All-American at West Virginia, had always saved his heaviest guns for the moments of truth. With nothing at stake, he was a competent basketball player doing a workmanlike job. With the chips down, he was a ball of fire.

It happened in the 1962 N.B.A. playoffs, when he averaged more than 32 points a game, two more than he averaged during the regular season. It happened in the 1961 playoffs, when West, then a rookie, averaged 23 points a game, nearly six points better than his regular season mark. And it happened in college, for, although West never won a national scoring title, he once tied the N.C.A.A. tournament record of 160 points.

With Elgin Baylor, West gave Los Angeles a good one-two punch in 1961. In 1962 it was the best in the N.B.A. until January, when Baylor went into the army. The Lakers were on top of the standings at the time, and the experts predicted a team collapse, but West made them eat their words. As always, he rose to the occasion, inspiring his teammates by his great play and practically carrying them on his back to their first Western Division title since George Mikan's time.

It was a fantastic job, pulled off by a fantastic young man. At 175 pounds, West is one of the two or three lightest men in the N.B.A. Pound for pound, he has clearly succeeded the incomparable Cousy as the greatest little man in the business.

One of West's most amazing characteristics is his ability to ignore his physical troubles. He has a bad sinus condition and is injury-prone, yet he rarely misses a game. He played in all of the Lakers' 79 regular-season contests in 1961 and 75 of their 80 in 1962, and didn't miss a playoff game either year. He looked like death warmed over after every one of them.

At the end of a ball game, West seems on the verge of an asthma attack. Because of his sinus condition, the result of four nose breaks, he gasps as if every breath will be his last when he's very tired. Most of the time he refuses to admit there's anything wrong. He sits in front of his locker, his eyes bleary from smoke and his breath coming in agonizing groans, and insists that he never felt better in his life.

The only time his wife, Janey, a former West Virginia co-ed, ever heard him complain was on a February day in 1961, when he left the house sniffling.

"Listen to the game if you want to," he said, "but you won't hear anything about me. I've got such a bad cold I won't be able to play."

But when he arrived at the Arena he learned that Baylor was out with the flu, so he put on a uniform. That night he played the full 48 minutes, scored 38 points, grabbed 15 rebounds and led the Lakers to a 121–116 victory over Wilt Chamberlain and the Philadelphia Warriors. It was a typical West performance and Janey, who knew her husband, didn't miss any of it.

Jerry started out the 1961–62 season by spraining his ankle the first week of the season. He did it again a couple of weeks later, then, before he was fully recovered, went into another game with the Warriors against the better judgment of Fred Schaus, the Lakers' coach. The first thing Jerry did was steal the ball from Chamberlain, gallop down the floor without a noticeable limp and shoot a basket. He went on to score 36 points that night while holding Tom Gola, his opponent, down to 19.

Two nights later, when West had fallen heavily and landed on his right hand and left foot, he had to be helped off the floor. Chick Hearn, the Lakers' radio announcer, told his listeners, "There goes Jerry West. You won't see him back in the lineup for some time."

Two minutes later, Jerry was back in the ball game and the astounded Hearn was saying over the mike, "If I hadn't seen it, I wouldn't have believed it possible."

On the following night, the Lakers played Syracuse in Portland, Oregon, and West sprained his ankle again. After the trainer had taped it up, he wanted to go back into the game, but Schaus wouldn't let him. So Jerry sat on the bench, wondering what Janey would think after she heard that he was out for the rest of the game.

Just to be sure Hearn would announce that he was O.K., West forced himself to walk off the floor without a limp. Then he collapsed with pain in the locker room.

Baylor is the big scorer of the Lakers, but West is the quarterback, the man who makes the club click. He has always idealized Cousy, and he plays much the same type of game. He has the same determination, the same killer instinct, the same drive. And like Cousy, it is West who carries the ball up-court, puts it into play from out of bounds, provides inspiration and calls the play patterns.

He knows them like the back of his hand, for he has been using the same patterns for years. Schaus was his coach at West Virginia, and the two went into the N.B.A. together.

The son of an electrician, Jerry grew up in a two-story frame house in Chelyan, about 35 miles from Charleston, West Virginia. Chelyan is so small that it has no post office of its own, so it's served by the one at nearby Cabin Creek. When Jerry first gained fame at West Virginia, he was dubbed "the hick from Cabin Creek," a title which still stays with him, even though he is now a sophisticated big city boy.

His brother David, 15 years older, who was later killed in Korea, first taught Jerry the fundamentals of basketball. Jerry grew up playing the game, and won local fame as the star of the Consolidated East Bank High School team, which he led to a state title in his senior year. West scored 926 points in 27 games, including 39 in the finals of the championship tournament. East Bank didn't lose a game that year.

It was after the title was clinched that Jerry got his first real taste of adulation, and he didn't like it. A modest youngster, all he wanted to do was play basketball and be left alone. But everyone in the area went crazy after East Bank won the crown. The mayor changed the name of the town to West Bank for a day in honor of Jerry, and people Jerry had never met before flocked around to shake his hand and pat his back.

Worse, scouts and coaches descended like locusts on the house in Chelyan to talk to him about college. He got offers from all over the country, many of them so lucrative that he didn't think they were serious. The phone rang so much that his mother took the receiver off the hook.

One day she said, "Son, I wish you would make up your

mind where you're going, so we can have some peace around here."

"That's the trouble," he said, "I can't decide."

"Well," she said, "if it was up to me, I'd go to college in the state where I'm best known."

That did it. Jerry picked West Virginia the next day. He probably would have anyhow sooner or later. He had met and liked both Schaus and Rod (Hot Rod) Hundley, then an All-American player and one of the big stars of the country. Hundley today is a Lakers teammate of West, and the two are still close friends.

Jerry's life at West Virginia was one triumph after another. His freshman team was undefeated as Jerry averaged nearly 20 points a game. He had a glaring weakness, for he did all his driving and faking to the right and was an uncertain ball-handler.

"Work on your ball handling," Schaus told him. "And try to do things from the left as well as the right."

Jerry practiced all summer, and was a much better ball-handler when he returned. But it took him years to become the finished two-way player he is today.

He made the West Virginia varsity easily in his sophomore year, and was the big man of a team that won 14 in a row, lost one, then won 12 more in succession. Although West Virginia lost to Manhattan in the first round of the N.C.A.A., the Mountaineers led all the nation's polls as the best team in the country.

The "hick from Cabin Creek" made All-America in his junior year, and by the time he was a senior, he was the most famous young man in West Virginia. The governor wanted to meet him, so Jerry went to the executive mansion in Charleston. When he walked into the outer office, he said to the secretary, "I'm Jerry West. I have an appointment with the governor."

"You don't have to tell me who you are," she replied. "You're better known than he is."

Mobbed wherever he went, Jerry was no happier in the college spotlight than he had been in high school. He couldn't venture out of his room at Morgantown without being surrounded by admirers. After a while, he went to the movies to hide out. It was the only place where he could find peace.

Although West Virginia failed to win the N.C.A.A. Tournament, the Mountaineers came as close as possible in 1959, the year Jerry tied the scoring record. After winning the Southern Conference title, they marched all the way to the finals before losing to California by a point. West led both teams in scoring and rebounds, and was named the tournament's most valuable player.

He was back on the All-America team in 1960, a year in which he again made life miserable for the opposition. He hit his peak against Kentucky in the Kentucky Invitation Tournament at Lexington. He broke his nose in the first half, and the Wildcats thought he was out of action for the night. But he came back to score 19 points in the second half for a total of 36, and West Virginia won the tournament.

After the game, Adolph Rupp, the Wildcats' coach, said, "I've seen a million basketball players in my time, and this kid is one of the best."

Later, Oscar Robertson, hailed as the best college player of the year all over the country, was asked, "Do you think Jerry West is the second best?"

"He's probably the best," Robertson replied.

When the season was finally over, Rupp gave West the supreme accolade. "I'm sure glad that boy is graduating," the veteran coach said. "If he weren't, we'd gladly give him an honorary degree just to get him out of there."

Jerry went to Rome as co-captain with Robertson of the American Olympic basketball team in 1960. There was no doubt about his next move on his return. The Lakers had hired Schaus for the sole purpose of having the coach who knew Jerry best. Besides, Schaus had also had Hundley as a college player, and they knew he could help Hundley, too.

West, who had married Janey Kane as a senior, signed a two-year contract at $20,000. The couple took an apartment in the Los Angeles suburb of Westdale.

Jerry was an immediate N.B.A. star. By the end of the first month of his rookie season, he was third in scoring, behind only Chamberlain and Baylor. Then he sprained an ankle in Boston and dropped back, but ended up one of the highest scorers among backcourt men. He played 25 minutes in the All-Star game and made the All-League team.

Good as he was in 1961, he was even better in 1962. For the first time, he really mastered the art of doing everything from both sides, instead of only from the right. As a two-way player, he became one of the most dangerous men in the league, and more like Cousy than ever.

He has the best jump shot of any small man in the N.B.A. His lack of height is a handicap, but he can still outjump men five to eight inches taller. He finished fifth in the scoring race, behind only the giants of the league. His 2310 points were the most by any backcourt player.

Nobody minimizes West's value to the Lakers, but there

was never better proof of it than when he was forced to miss five games in mid-season. The club lost four of them. It picked up only when Jerry was back in action.

A sensible young man in almost all other ways, West is one of the most superstitious characters in the league. When his club wins, he wears the same clothes every day until it loses. He always walks out of the locker room third in line, although he doesn't care who is ahead or behind him. And he has a chewing gum habit which can be compared only to that of Eddie Collins, the old-time baseball star, who always went to bat with his gum stuck in a wad on the peak of his cap.

Before each game, Jerry breaks a piece of gum in half, putting one half into his mouth and setting the other on top of his locker. In the Lakers' dressing room in Los Angeles, the top of West's locker is covered with half-sticks of chewing gum by the end of the season.

Jerry is a long way from Cabin Creek, where his folks still live, in more ways than one. He is now a solid citizen of Westdale, and knows now to take advantage of the fame that once was a source of such annoyance to him. He has augmented his income with endorsements, appearances and business interests. And, along with Don Drysdale of the baseball Dodgers and Les Richter of the football Rams, he runs a summer camp for boys into which he intends to put more and more time as the years go on.

But right now he's concentrating on basketball. The most exciting little man since Cousy, Jerry has a lot of records to catch up with. Since he seems to be at his best when hurt or sick, injury or illness might be the last things that will stop him. He's the only athlete in history who doesn't need good health to keep going.

16

DOLPH SCHAYES

Syracuse sports fans hope that Dolph Schayes, basketball's Iron Horse, will go on forever. The big bushy-haired star, highest scorer and first 15,000-point man in N.B.A. history, is all that keeps major league basketball in Syracuse. When Schayes retires, the Nats will almost surely go to a larger city.

Even Danny Biasone, their loyal local proprietor, is about ready to concede that they must move elsewhere some day, but he won't consider the idea until Schayes is through. When some of the other club owners tried to pressure him into moving to Philadelphia to replace the Warriors, who switched from there to San Francisco at the end of the 1962 season, Biasone flatly refused.

"I'll fight to keep Syracuse in the league as long as my money and Schayes hold out," he said.

If Biasone's money holds out, the Nats may be in Syracuse for some time, for Schayes still seems to have several years of top-flight basketball left in his huge system. The

Dolph Schayes

six-foot, eight-inch forward finished his fourteenth season in 1962 and observed his thirty-fourth birthday in May, but the end of his magnificent career is nowhere in sight. He's the oldest man in the game in point of uninterrupted service, and the most durable in its history.

From the beginning of the 1949 season until the day after Christmas in 1961, when a broken cheekbone forced him out of action, Schayes missed only three games. Between February 17, 1952, and December 26, 1961, he piled up a record total of 705 consecutive games, not counting playoffs.

This was only one of the records which Schayes held at the end of the 1962 season. He and Bob Cousy of the Boston Celtics were the only players chosen for every N.B.A. All-Star game, although a broken wrist kept Dolph out of the 1952 classic and he had to wear a protective mask in the 1962 contest. He made either the first or second All-Star team 13 years in succession. By the end of 1962, he had scored more points, played more games and minutes, and had the most field goals, free throws, rebounds and personal fouls of anyone in the business.

In the all-time list of N.B.A. stars, Schayes's name comes first. Although he broke into the pros at a time when scores were much lower, his average point production is close to 20 a game. Soon after the beginning of the 1963 season, Schayes will play in his 1000th N.B.A. game. This figure is out of reach of everyone else in basketball at the present time.

Schayes is the most accurate big man who ever lived, the only one as effective from outside as under the basket. He is the ideal all-round player, for he has fingertip control of the ball from a distance and is a rough competitor in the bruising battles for the ball under the boards. He is high among the all-time rebounders, yet the most deadly foul shooter in the game today. Except for Bill Sharman of the Boston Celtics, Schayes is the best foul shot who ever lived.

Like Sharman, Schayes has a soft touch and, like Sharman, he can sink the ball from almost any reasonable distance. In the N.B.A., they call Schayes the "Rainbow Kid" because his long shots describe a high arc like a rainbow. Most of them swish through the basket without touching the sides, for Schayes rarely tries to carom the ball off the backboard or the rim.

No man in the game has done as much to hold one team together as Schayes has for the Nats. He led them to the 1955 world's championship and has kept them in the playoffs for years. No all-time N.B.A. team is complete without him, for he is one of the greatest stars basketball has ever known.

Yet he showed such little promise as a college player that the New York Knickerbockers, who had first crack at him, made him only a token offer, then refused to raise it when the chips were down. It was a decision they have bitterly regretted ever since.

"If we hadn't passed up Schayes," said Ned Irish, the Knicks' president, "we might have been the Yankees of basketball instead of the patsies."

The Knickerbockers have never won an N.B.A. championship.

Still, they could hardly be blamed for not getting hysterical over Schayes. The youth, who graduated as an aeronautical engineer from New York University at the age of nineteen, had been a mediocre basketball player there. Only

his size kept him on the team at all, for he was far from an
All-American and not even the top star of his own team.
He was just a big kid who lacked the competitive spark, a
young giant who let himself get pushed around by everyone
he faced. If he had been a few inches shorter, no professional team would have looked twice at him.

Howard Cann, Schayes's own college coach, didn't think
much of his chances. In 1957, Cann left Dolph off his personal all-time team, selected from the boys whom he had
coached during his 35-year career.

"Schayes is unquestionably the best player ever turned
out at N.Y.U.," Cann said at the time, "but I picked the
men on the basis of what they had done at college. Dolph
wasn't particularly outstanding here. I didn't think he was
rugged or aggressive enough to survive in pro ball."

Schayes, however, had nature going for him. In 1948,
six-feet, eight-inch kids weren't exactly coming out of the
woodwork. Furthermore, there were two pro leagues, the
Basketball Association of America (now the N.B.A.) and
the National Basketball League, competing against each
other.

The Knicks, who had territorial rights to Schayes, made
him a routine salary offer of $6000. Dolph might have ac-
cepted, but Syracuse, then in the N.B.L., upped the ante to
$7500. When the Knicks failed to match the figure, Schayes
signed with the Nats.

Al Cervi, a bantam battler who made up in aggressiveness for his lack of height, was the Nats' player-coach. For
the first two months of the season, Cervi fought Dolph's
battles for him, pushing the kid aside and squaring off
against whoever his tormentor happened to be. Eventually, Cervi lost patience with his placid rookie.

"Look," he said to Schayes one day, "you're a big boy now. It's high time you fought your own battles. Next time somebody belts you, belt back."

All Schayes had to do was belt back a few times before his rivals stopped picking on him. He was one of the biggest men in the league and well on his way toward becoming one of the strongest. Once he realized his own strength, he would be dynamite to fool with. No one knew this better than Cervi. The Syracuse coach not only set this sleeping giant on fire, but did more than anyone else to make a great basketball player out of him.

While Cervi preached aggressiveness out of one side of his mouth, he preached hard work out of the other.

"Size alone won't make a star out of you," the Nats' coach told Schayes, "but size, plus desire, plus competitive spirit, plus endless practice can make you the greatest player who ever lived."

Cervi wasn't just talking; he really believed it. After a while, he had Schayes believing it, too. Dolph worked on every phase of the game, with particular emphasis on shooting. He practiced morning, noon and night, on off days as well as on game days, patiently repeating every move, constantly battling for perfection.

In order to improve his foul shooting, Dolph fitted a 14-inch basket into the regulation 18-inch hoop, and fired the ball through that for hours. He became so accurate that he could put the ball through the smaller basket without touching the sides. Eventually, the regular basket looked big to him. It still does.

Syracuse moved into the N.B.A. in 1949 when the two leagues combined. Schayes was ready for the transformation into basketball's fastest company. He still had much to learn, but he was already the guts of the Nats' team. He finished sixth in scoring in a league so cumbersome that it required three divisions to take care of 17 teams. With Schayes their only man among the first 25 scorers, the Nats won the Eastern Division title and carried the Minneapolis Lakers through six games of the final round before losing the championship. Only George Mikan outscored Schayes during those playoffs.

This was the tipoff on what was to come in the immediate future. The Lakers were the best, but Syracuse was the most consistently second best. The Nats won three Eastern Division crowns and one league title in six years, with Schayes always the key man on the team. He never led the league in scoring, but, except for one year, he was never lower than seventh, and usually fifth or higher. No Syracuse teammate was ever close to him.

He was one of the first of the great rebounders. In 1950, he grabbed 35 rebounds in a game against Philadelphia, the highest total made in one game up to that time. A year later, he became the first man to collect over 1000 when he set a league record of 1060.

For years his accuracy at the foul line was challenged or exceeded only by Bill Sharman. In 1957 Schayes set a league record when he sank 625 fouls. It was broken in later years, but Dolph regained his crown in 1961 when he dumped in a new record total of 680. His foul shots are not spectacular—simply deadly accurate. The ball floats through the hoop with a bare flick of one of Schayes's long fingers.

This fingertip control is the result of an injury. When he broke his right wrist in 1952, Schayes had to change his style. He had always shot from the foul line by holding the ball firmly in both hands. With his arm in a plastic cast, this was impossible, so he got into the habit of flicking his shots. He became so good at it that he never went back to his old method.

Schayes takes a terrible beating in every game. Opponents know that he is the Syracuse team, and they are constantly trying to get him out of there. He has learned to protect himself while barreling toward the basket like a freight train. An expert at the use of elbows, hips and shoulders, he deals out plenty of punishment himself, but his body is a mass of bruises after every game.

This doesn't bother him. "I like to get hit," he once said. "It means I'm getting in close enough for good shots."

This must have come as a surprise to boyhood friends who grew up with Dolph in New York's Bronx. He was a timid youngster who dreaded physical contact, much to his father's annoyance. The elder Schayes, who stood six feet, four inches, was a frustrated boxer, and for a while he had vague hopes that his son might succeed where he had failed. There never was a chance. Dolph wouldn't even put on boxing gloves, much less throw a punch.

But he loved basketball. He was awkward and ungainly, but as the biggest boy in the neighborhood he had plenty of chance to play. Sometimes the kids climbed through a window to play in the nearby N.Y.U. gym. More than once, Dolph was thrown out of there by the coach, Howard Cann, for whom he later played.

At Creston Junior High School, Dolph made his first formal team, and he played wherever he went to school after that. His size alone got him by in high school, where his lack of aggressiveness was not a heavy drawback. He made the De Witt Clinton High School team at thirteen.

Two years later, nearly as tall as his father, he was one of the biggest schoolboy athletes in New York.

The whole Clinton team was offered scholarships to Purdue in 1944, when the five varsity members graduated from high school together. But two of the boys went into the service, and Dolph, who was too young, entered N.Y.U. He played his first college game two days before he began classes. At that time, freshmen were eligible for varsity competition because World War II was still in progress.

Dolph scored well from the start, but his lack of competitive spirit was all too obvious even then. He was all right until he got hit, then he went into a shell. He had a fine set shot—which he has retained to this day—but an aggressive opponent could handle him easily.

Vince Boryla, later an N.B.A. star and coach of the Knicks, was then playing for Notre Dame. One night at Madison Square Garden in 1945, he faced Schayes in a game between the Irish and N.Y.U. As soon as Boryla found that Dolph wouldn't fight back, he made mincemeat out of the scared kid from the Bronx. When the game was over, Notre Dame had won an easy victory and Boryla had 16 points to Schayes's 3.

Years later, when he was coaching the Knicks, Boryla said one day, "Schayes is the most underrated man in the N.B.A. I still can't believe this is the same guy I outplayed so in college."

N.Y.U. did well enough in Dolph's freshman year to go to the finals of the N.C.A.A., losing the title to Oklahoma A. & M. And three years later, when Schayes was a senior, the Violet five won 22 and lost 2.

"If Schayes had been less gun-shy," one of his teammates said later, "we might have gone undefeated. He was the biggest man on the team and the best scorer, but he simply wouldn't fight for his rights."

When someone once asked Schayes what made him change so quickly from a college lamb into a professional lion, he replied, "Cervi was the motivating factor because he told me frankly that if I didn't wake up I couldn't live in this league. Some people thought I was just afraid of getting hurt, but it wasn't that. It wasn't lack of desire to win either. I wasn't frightened, and I certainly wanted to win. Maybe I was just plain lazy. It was too much work to fight back and I didn't want to bother."

Actually, Schayes continued to lack initiative for years. He could have made a small fortune on outside activities around Syracuse, where he is the most popular figure in town. He turned down countless opportunities to go into business or to do work that would require him simply to go out and meet people. For many years, he did nothing but practice basketball in the off-season. He spent part of his summers playing for teams in the Borscht Circuit of the Catskill Mountains, but this was the only extra money he made for some time.

However, he is now part owner of Camp Valcour in Plattsburg, N.Y., and he also has finally developed some business interests around Syracuse, where he lives in a large, modern home with his wife and children. The Nats pay him about $25,000 a year, and expect to continue to do so for a long time.

Dolph himself has no more idea than anyone else how long he can keep going in the pro league. It won't be his fault if he fails to last much longer. He is a scrupulously clean athlete, who takes perfect care of himself. He gets plenty of sleep and exercise, eats well and with care, and lives up to the strictest of training rules both in and out of the season.

Some experts think he'll go on for some years because of his unusually low pulse rate. In repose, his pulse is 48, much less than that of the average person of his age. According to the Nats' team physician, Dr. Max E. Rifkin, this explains his tremendous staying power.

"Schayes carries fatigue better than other players," Dr. Rifkin says, "because his heart does the same work with less effort. He actually gets stronger as exertion accelerates his pulse."

Dolph is as loyal to Syracuse as Biasone. He has been living there since he joined the Nats as a youngster still a few months short of his twentieth birthday. His wife, the former Naomi Gross, whom he married in 1952, was a music student at Syracuse University and his children were all born there.

"I haven't lived in New York for years," he says, "and now I've got no desire to. The people here have been wonderful to me, and I consider this more my home than New York ever was."

Actually, he once came very close to going back to New York, although he wasn't aware of it at the time. In 1950, the Nats seemed on the verge of folding, and Ned Irish tried to buy the club just to get Schayes. Biasone appealed to the people of Syracuse to save the franchise. They responded by buying 150 bonds at $1000 each, and the Nats stayed where they were.

A year or so later, Irish offered three top men—Dick McGuire, Harry Gallatin and Nat (Sweetwater) Clifton— for Schayes. It was a tempting deal, but Biasone refused. "They'd run me out of town if I traded Schayes," he said

at the time. They would certainly run him out of town if he
traded Schayes today.

Dolph's proudest possession is a basketball given him the
night he scored his 15,000th point in January of 1960. The
Nats were playing the Celtics at Philadelphia when Schayes
curved a long shot gracefully in from twenty feet out during
the third period. The game was stopped while the ball was
given him, and everyone on both teams crowded around to
congratulate him.

Then the battle resumed and Schayes went on as if nothing unusual had happened. So did everyone else, and Dolph
was his normal black-and-blue self when he got into the
locker room afterwards.

As his teammates congratulated him again, he sat quietly
in front of his locker. "It won't be long before someone else
does it," he remarked.

"Probably not," one of the others said, "but you'll always be the first."

Schayes nodded, and smiled.

Then he showered and dressed, and left with the others,
looking forward to his second 15,000. There are those who
think he might make it.

Bob Cousy

17

BOB COUSY

W HEN BOB COUSY announced in the spring of 1962 that he would become a college coach after one more year of professional basketball, he served notice that the most remarkable career the game has ever known was nearing its end. When Cousy hangs up his sneakers for good, it will mark the end of an era. The gap he leaves will never be filled.

This is not simply because Cousy is the best little man of all time, or because he has been the spirit of the Boston Celtics since 1950, or because he is the finest play-maker the game has produced, or because he can perform feats of magic with a basketball in his hands. Nor is it simply because he is the only one who has made the All-League team in each of his years in the N.B.A., and the only one who played in every All-Star game. Nor is it even simply because he is the ideal basketball player, the man by whom all others are judged.

It is because Cousy gave class and dignity to a sport which had never had much of either before he came

around. At the time Cousy joined the Celtics, pro basketball was only a few years removed from its tank-town days.
It had never had a big league, and wasn't sure how a big
league should operate. Most of the teams, including the
Celtics, had financial troubles, and nobody knew how long
the league would last.

The game lacked pride and self-confidence. Its only hero
was George Mikan, but, big as he was, Mikan couldn't
carry the whole N.B.A. on his back. Thanks to him, Minneapolis was a solid franchise, but Minneapolis couldn't
live alone. Besides, Mikan was such a tremendous man—
six feet, ten—that the average person couldn't really iden-
tify with him. The fans needed someone nearer their own
size.

Cousy was the man. At six, one and a half, he was of
average size, small only by basketball standards. The mar-
vels of his ball handling, his dash and fire and killer instinct,
his leadership qualities, and his ability to outplay even the
great Mikan, captured everyone's imagination. More important, Cousy had such intense pride that he infused everyone around him with it. Others might apologize for the
N.B.A.; Cousy insisted there was nothing to apologize for.

"When you speak of the N.B.A., you don't call it the
'pro game,'" he used to say. "You call it 'big league,' because that's what it is."

Cousy helped to make it so in fact as well as in name.
From the beginning, he fought anything that smacked of
cheapness or the bush leagues. He demanded that the
N.B.A. pay enough for officials to get the best available
referees, that the teams travel well and stay in first-class
hotels, that the small towns in the league be replaced by
big ones. For years, he served unofficially as a one-man
grievance committee. A player with a legitimate complaint

found a friend in Cousy, who was never afraid to go to bat for a man who failed to get a square deal.

By the same token, he insisted that the players act like big leaguers. If a club got the worst of it in its dealings with an athlete, Cousy talked to the offender, making sure that he played fair with his owner. He quietly solved problems so ticklish that there appeared to be no solution. He knew nobody else could. He was the only one who had the respect of all the owners and all the players.

Inevitably, Cousy got into trouble with the league front office. For years, he and Maurice Podoloff, the N.B.A. president, were at swords' points, but this never bothered Cousy. He battled for a players' association because he knew it was a fight in which he would have to take the lead if the players were to win. The association was finally formed in the spring of 1957, a triumph which Cousy still considers one of the great thrills of his life. He fought for the pension plan which now exists, and for many of the other benefits which players take for granted today.

Cousy became the symbol of professional basketball, players' player, coaches' player, writers' player and fans' player. He was the biggest name in the game, and the easiest man to interview. He was—and is—in greater demand by outsiders for personal appearances and endorsements than anyone else in the game. When President Eisenhower met a panel of athletes to discuss a physical fitness program, Cousy represented professional basketball. He has traveled all over the world lecturing, giving demonstrations and spreading the good name of the game he loves.

And, throughout his fabulous career, he continued to play magnificent basketball. He holds almost all of the league records for assists, for he is the greatest passer and play-maker who ever lived. Although not noted as a great scorer, he stands among the top five in the league's all-time records. In a dozen years of big league basketball, he has averaged nearly 20 points a game.

As a team leader, he is in a class by himself. He is one of the few athletes in any sport who, by his very presence in the lineup, can perk up a whole team.

"The thing we'll miss most when Cousy is gone," says Coach Red Auerbach of the Celtics, "is the inspiration that he provides. He makes us click. Time and time again, I've seen him pull the team together when things went wrong. It's like having another coach out on the floor."

Cousy's feats are innumerable and, in some cases, almost unbelievable. He once scored 50 points in a playoff game at a time when this was close to the league record for one game. He has pulled over a hundred losing games out of the fire in the last few minutes of play.

No one knows better than he what he means to the team. When the Celtics had trouble in the first four games of the playoff finals against the Hawks in 1960, Cousy, who had had a poor series, said, "I'm ruining these playoffs. If I don't do better, I'll have to bench myself."

He scored 21 key points, almost all in the second half, and the Celtics won the fifth game. Then, after the Hawks evened the series, Cousy went wild in the finale, scoring 19 points, piling up 14 assists and, despite his lack of height, even getting more than his share of rebounds off the backboard.

One of the things that makes Cousy great is his ability to do everything well. The records show him on top only as a play-maker, but, on a given day, Cousy could outplay everyone else in some department of the game. He might be the top scorer one night, the top foul shooter another, the top rebounder a third.

His ball handling is superb. He can pass the ball off from any angle, out-fake everyone in the league, shift the ball from hand to hand behind his back, look one way and pass another. As a stunt man, he is in a class by himself. Even the Harlem Globetrotters, who specialize in the unusual, marvel at some of the things Cousy can do.

But it is as a clutch man that he stands head and shoulders above his fellows, regardless of height or weight. "With Cousy in there," a rival coach said a few years ago, "the Celtics are never licked. The only time I feel safe is when we have a ten-point lead with five seconds to go."

Years after he went back to college coaching, Joe Lapchick, the former Knickerbockers coach, told a writer, "There never was a basketball player like Bob Cousy going down the stretch—never—not anywhere, any time."

Always primarily a second-half scorer, Cousy came through so often in clutches that it became routine when he took charge of a game in the last few minutes. Boston fans and players alike adopted the slogan, "Have no fear, Cousy's here," and Bob rarely failed them.

Yet he was shrewd enough to know that it takes five men to make a basketball team, and they can't all be Cousys.

"Five guys like me would get murdered in this league," he told me when I worked with him on his life story, *Basketball Is My Life*, published in 1958. "If you don't have that big guy who can grab rebounds, you're dead."

He was frustrated, but not upset because he played on no championship teams during the first half of his career. Cousy knew as well as Auerbach that the Celtics had everything but a rebound man. And when they finally found one in Bill Russell, Cousy was the first to realize that they were on the verge of an unprecedented golden era. He predicted

their long reign over the N.B.A. in 1957, after they won
their first title. By 1962, they had won five titles in six
years, four of them in a row.

For years, there were stories out of Boston that Cousy
and Auerbach were at each other's throats, that Cousy resented Auerbach's failure to draft him when he graduated
from Holy Cross in 1950, and that Cousy objected to Auerbach's refusal to acknowledge Cousy's greatness. There
wasn't a shred of truth in any of these rumors. Cousy and
Auerbach had a routine player-coach relationship for several years, with Auerbach giving the orders and Cousy
taking them. Eventually, they became the close friends they
are today. They have made several trips abroad together,
and each is the other's biggest booster.

Despite a fabulous college record, Cousy wasn't drafted
by the Celtics, who had first crack at him. As the last-place
team in their division in 1949, they had their choice of college players all over the country. Auerbach, who had just
become the coach, wanted the biggest man he could find,
so he selected Bowling Green's Charley Share, who stood
six feet, eleven inches. Cousy was drafted by Ben Kerner's
Tri-Cities team.

Although he didn't know it, Bob belonged to three teams
before he put on a uniform. Kerner traded him to the
Chicago Stags for Gene Vance, but the Stags promptly
folded. A league meeting was held to distribute the players, and eventually only Cousy, Andy Phillip and Max
Zaslofsky were left, with one each to go to the Celtics, the
Knickerbockers and the Warriors.

They all wanted Zaslofsky, a proven star and a four-time
member of the All-League team. Phillip was the second
choice and Cousy the last. The argument lasted far into the
night, and was settled only when the three teams agreed to

pull the names of the players out of a hat. Walter Brown, the Celtics' owner, was the first to draw, and he got Cousy.

Years later, Brown said, "How lucky can you get? We didn't deserve him."

When Cousy first reported to the Celtics, he was a fancy ball-handler and a good shooter, but he had plenty to learn, especially about defensive play, at which he was very weak. "Of course, I didn't call him great," Auerbach says. "He wasn't. It was as simple as that."

But when Cousy had mastered all there was to master, the coach was the first to capitulate. "Is Cousy great?" he says today. "Why, there's nobody close to him."

Even Ben Kerner, who rarely agrees with Auerbach about anything, admits he's right about Cousy. The man who traded Cousy off said not long ago, "There's no question about it. Cousy is the greatest player of all time."

Slater Martin, the only little man who ever could cope with Cousy—and he couldn't do it consistently—often talks about their battles when Martin played for Minneapolis and later St. Louis. "Of course Cousy was the best," he says. "Nobody was in a class with him. I got a bigger kick out of holding him down than scoring myself."

Perhaps the most impressive tribute came from Oswald Tower, who edited the *Basketball Guide* for half a century. "I've seen them all," he once said. "No one approaches Cousy."

Bob was born in the slums of New York's East Side on August 9, 1928. His mother, although American-born, was brought up in France and could not speak English. His father was from Alsace-Lorraine. They came to America a few months before Bob was born, and spoke nothing but French at home. As a result, that was the only language Bob knew until he started going to school at age five.

On top of that, he had a slight speech defect, which was never completely cured. Although poised and articulate today, he still rolls his r's and has occasional trouble with his l's. He can laugh at himself now, but as a kid growing up, he was very sensitive about his difficulty in speaking.

The Cousys moved to Long Island when Bob was eleven, and he spent his adolescent years in St. Albans. He first won basketball fame at Andrew Jackson High School, and was named captain of New York's All-Scholastic team in 1946. He entered Holy Cross that fall, and never returned to New York permanently.

Cousy lives in a big old house in Worcester, Massachusetts, where he went to college. During the basketball season, he commutes the 35 miles to Boston. This distressed both Walter Brown and Red Auerbach for years, because they were afraid he would get into an accident or be delayed by car trouble of some kind. In a dozen years, however, Cousy was late for only one game and didn't miss a single practice session at which he was expected.

The Celtics are the highest-paid team in the league, and Cousy probably its highest-paid player. For years he accepted a comparatively small salary, for he knew that Brown was struggling to keep the team alive. At one point, the owner was a quarter of a million dollars in the red.

Cousy, being asked once why he didn't demand more money, replied, "Why should I? Walter lost a fortune on this club. If I tried to hold him up for a big raise, he might not be able to keep the team. When things get better, Walter will pay me more money. I'm not worried."

He had nothing to worry about. When the Celtics began to show a profit, Cousy shared in it. He and Brown have a bonus arrangement based on attendance, by which Bob can now make as much as $50,000 in a season.

A good businessman, he has a number of outside interests. With two partners, he runs Camp Graylag, a boys' camp in Pittsfield, New Hampshire. He is a partner in a successful insurance business in Worcester. He is employed on a retainer basis by several national companies which pay him well for the use of his name. And, of course, he gets his share of the endorsements and extras which are available to all top athletes.

His favorite off-season sport is now golf, although he once thought the game was too easy to present a challenge. He couldn't be blamed for this attitude. The first time he played, he broke 100 and had a hole-in-one. For years after that, tennis was his second favorite sport.

Unlike so many other great athletes, who refuse to believe they're through, Cousy is bowing gracefully out of basketball. He began to slow up in 1960, and was perfectly aggreeable when Auerbach suggested that he spend more time on the bench.

"We were lucky to have someone like Sam Jones to replace me," Cousy says. "He's one of the best backcourt men in the league, and one of the most accurate shooters I ever saw. We're better off with him in there than with me."

Although the day may come when Cousy will become a big league coach, he's looking forward to the next three years, when he will coach the Boston College basketball team.

"I'll miss the Celtics," he said after announcing his coming retirement. "Who wouldn't? But it's better to quit while you're ahead. I don't want to be a burden on anybody."

When he leaves in 1963, it will be Boston College's gain and the N.B.A.'s loss. The pro game never saw his like before—and probably never will again.

Elgin Baylor flies at basket.

18

ELGIN BAYLOR

Every great basketball player has a style of his own. Some seem to be working themselves to the bone, huffing and puffing and panting as they dash back and forth. Some seem to work hard only when they work, but to loaf when they pace themselves. And some—just a very few —are will-o'-the-wisps who never stop going at top speed, but glide along so smoothly that they hardly seem to be working at all. The smoothest of these is Elgin Baylor of the Los Angeles Lakers.

Baylor is the most graceful man in basketball. He floats down-court as though he were carrying his 225-pound, six-foot, five-inch body on ball bearings. There never seems to be a break in his stride, not even when he has to stop suddenly and shift direction. He even fakes with the grace of a ballet dancer.

Except for an occasional quick jerk of his head, caused by a neck twitch which comes only when he plays basketball, Baylor's whole body is a beautiful thing to watch, and the fact that he happens to be a remarkable basketball player makes it all the more beautiful.

A veteran observer, after watching him for the first time, said later, "Even if he never scored a basket, I'd rather watch this guy than anyone in the league. Nobody else has his style and rhythm. Nobody else makes this game look easier."

And few others have Baylor's ability to score points, or, for that matter, his ability to do any of the other things required on a basketball court. Baylor is the complete player. He can shoot, pass, dribble, call plays and feint, and he's murderous at the backboards. Except for the 1961–62 season, nearly half of which he spent in the army, he has had 1000 or more rebounds a year since 1958, when he first came into the N.B.A.

He's always near the top in almost all departments of the game. His army service spoiled a progressive improvement in his place among the league's scorers that might have carried him past even the great Wilt Chamberlain in 1962. In his rookie season, Baylor was fourth in scoring. In his second year, he was third. In his third season, he was second. He couldn't be first in his fourth season because he took part in only 48 games. Even with this handicap, he finished eighth. The seven men ahead of him all played in at least 75 of the 80 games on the regular schedule.

Baylor led his team in scoring and rebounds in all three of his full seasons, and in assists in two of them. Except for Wilt Chamberlain, he is the only long-term player in the league with a lifetime scoring average of over 30 points a game.

With Jerry West, he transformed the Lakers from league doormats to Western Division champions. He and his back-court partner came within minutes of upsetting the Celtics in the 1962 playoff finals. Even though he had to travel to Fort Lewis, Washington, several times to report back for army duty during the playoffs, Baylor was the high scorer in each of the seven games.

He hit an all-time peak in the fifth game of the Celtics' series when he scored 61 points to break Bob Pettit's championship playoff record of 50. And, after only four years, Baylor was among the top five playoff scorers in N.B.A. history.

He made the All-League first team four years in a row, and starred for the West team in four straight All-Star games. He smashed several scoring records as a rookie in the 1959 game, when he shared Most Valuable Player honors with Pettit, and will probably smash several more before he's through.

Baylor was considered by experts to be ready for the N.B.A. a year before he came into the league. When Leo Leavitt of the Globetrotters saw him at the University of Seattle in the spring of 1958, he declared, "Baylor is better than Chamberlain or Russell already. He can do more things than either. And he's got speed, stamina, strength and competitive spirit."

Six months later, Baylor was tearing the N.B.A. apart. He's still doing it. If it weren't for Chamberlain, he'd be the greatest scorer of all time.

In his first pro game he scored 25 points against the Cincinnati Royals, but this was only the beginning. He improved so steadily that he actually pulled his average up to 41 points a game at the season's halfway mark. Paul Seymour, the Syracuse coach, remarked after Baylor tore the Nats apart one night, "This kid is the best rookie I've ever seen." Just about everyone else in the league agreed.

Almost exactly a year after he entered the pro game,

Baylor broke what up to then had been one of the N.B.A.'s most elusive records, the one-game mark of 63 points set by Joe Fulks of Philadelphia in 1949. In a game against the Celtics in Minneapolis on November 8, 1959, Baylor piled up 64 points.

A year and a week after that, on November 15, 1960, against the Knickerbockers at Madison Square Garden, Baylor set another new mark when he shot 71 points, including a record total of 28 baskets from the floor. Just to show how thoroughly Baylor dominated that game, which the Lakers won, 123–108, Elgin had 25 rebounds, 11 more than anyone else on either team. He played in all but three minutes of the game, which was about average for him.

In common with so many other young N.B.A. stars, Baylor was considered the last hope to save a franchise. The Lakers, the proudest team in the league during George Mikan's era, had degenerated. With Mikan gone, there were no more championships, and after a while the Minneapolis fans went sour on them. In the 1957–58 season, the team lost almost $140,000.

Bob Short, the Lakers' owner, was desperately anxious to keep the club in Minneapolis. He had twice successfully staved off attempts to move it elsewhere, and he hoped that Baylor could keep the wolf permanently away from the door. In his eagerness to get Elgin, Short followed the young man all over the country in the spring of 1958.

Baylor, a two-year All-American by the time he was a junior at the University of Seattle, was in an unusual position. A transfer student from the College of Idaho, he had lost an academic year, and wasn't due to graduate with his original college class in 1958. This made him eligible for pro basketball.

Not a particularly good student, Baylor had no intention of spending another year in college, but couldn't make up his mind whether to play for the Globetrotters or the Lakers. Both romanced him like suitors after a beautiful girl.

When Baylor got married in the summer of 1958, with Chamberlain as his best man, he still hadn't decided. Chamberlain couldn't help him, since Wilt was in college himself, and would soon be faced with the same decision. It was Baylor's bride who finally got Elgin to accept the Lakers' offer. She didn't relish the life of a basketball widow, which is what she would have been if Baylor had joined the Globetrotters. He finally signed with Short for $20,000 a year.

Baylor led the Lakers, who had been last in 1958, to a tremendous season. The club was second to the Hawks in the Western Division, then beat them in the playoff semifinals to earn the right to face the Celtics in the finals. It was a dubious honor, for Boston won four straight games, but this hardly detracted from the Lakers' position as Western champions.

The Lakers' 1959 success on the court was reflected in the box office. To Short's delight, his team grossed $300,000, and there was every reason to expect it to stay in Minneapolis indefinitely. With Baylor on the club and Jerry West only a year away, Short saw a future as rosy as the glorious past.

But the Lakers' owner, as it turned out, had been overconfident. Even though Baylor had another great year in 1960, again leading the team into the playoffs, Minneapolis apparently didn't want basketball after all. The fans stayed away in droves, and Short dropped over $100,000.

That did it. With pressure from the league to move, and an opportunity to take over the lush Los Angeles territory, Short threw in the towel. He shifted the franchise to the West Coast, and has been making money with it ever since. So has Baylor, whose salary is now over $30,000 a year, a figure he wouldn't have dared dream of in his poverty-stricken boyhood.

Elgin was born and brought up in the slums of Washington, D. C., where his biggest problem was school and his principal pleasure basketball. A poor student in the classroom, he made a fetish of learning everything he could about basketball. Big for his age, he was never satisfied to play with boys who made the game easy for him. He was always looking for older, stronger, bigger and better players than he.

"In grade school, I monkeyed around with high school kids," he recalls. "In high school, I wanted to play with fellows of college age. In that way, I always had to extend myself."

Even when he left Phelps Vocational High School in his junior year, Baylor continued to play basketball. He had a job in a furniture store, but he considered this only a sideline. His life was basketball, and he never intended to be away from the game for any length of time.

At his mother's insistence, he returned to school after working a year, entering Spingarn High School in Washington, where he made the national schoolboy All-American team in 1954. Because his marks were poor, there was no great rush of college scouts to his door, but a friend got him a basketball scholarship at the College of Idaho in Cardwell, and he started there that fall.

He was at Cardwell for a year, just long enough to average 31 points a game and make the small college All-American team. The school was so small that freshmen were eligible for the varsity, and he would have played four years if he had remained there. One of his teammates was R. C. Owens, later a great end for the San Francisco Forty-Niners football team.

When Baylor had a chance to shift to the University of Seattle, he grabbed it because it put him into big-time college basketball. He didn't enter until February of 1955, since he was ineligible for the varsity anyhow. He spent that winter playing for the Westside Fords, an A.A.U. team coached by Johnny O'Brien, a former Seattle star. Baylor led the league in scoring, averaging 33 points a game, while O'Brien smoothed off some of the rough edges of his play.

During the 1956–57 season, Baylor's first as a Seattle basketball player, he was the hottest college kid west of the Mississippi. That time he was on the real All-American team, for, all by himself, he had made Seattle a national power. In 1958 he was the Helms Foundation's player-of-the-year, and again made All-American. And, except for Oscar Robertson, he was the highest college scorer in the country.

The possibility of remaining another year in college to get his degree never occurred to him. "Why kid myself?" he said later. "I'm no student. Professional basketball is what I was meant for, so why put it off any longer?"

Always a little worried over his nervous head twitch, he thought he ought to do something about it after turning pro, so he consulted a neurologist. When the doctor learned the twitch came only while Baylor was playing basketball, he told Elgin to forget it. Today, it's the most famous gesture in the game. Lakers' fans now look for their star to tuck his head close to his shoulder with occasional jerks while he runs up and down the court.

Never especially race-conscious, Baylor accepted occasional restrictions as a matter of course for years. But soon after he joined the Lakers in 1958, he was badly upset when he and other Negroes were shut out of a hotel when the Lakers went to Charlotte, N.C., for a game with the Celtics.

"If that happens again, I won't play," Baylor told Short.

A month later it did happen again, this time in Charleston, W. Va., where the Lakers and the Royals had a game. The team then went to a Negro motel to spend the night, but there still was no place where Elgin could eat with his mates. After dinner, Coach Johnny Kundla found Baylor sitting on the bed in his room with his head in his hands.

"Are you sick?" Kundla asked.

"No," Baylor replied. "I'm embarrassed—and all torn up inside."

True to his threat, he refused to dress for the game. He sat on the bench in street clothes that night, watching the Lakers lose to the Royals. It was the last time the Lakers have ever played in the Jim Crow belt. To avoid similar incidents, N.B.A. teams almost never play there any more.

This suits Baylor very well, for he is not by nature a rebel, and he dislikes being the cause of anything that smacks of controversy. All he wants to do is play basketball, and that's all the Lakers want him to do.

He has a wonderful time at it, and sometimes finds it hard to believe that he has arrived where he is. "Imagine collecting all this money for having so much fun," he told a friend recently. "Why, I love this game enough so I'd play for nothing if I didn't have anyone but myself to think about."

He probably would, too.

19

BILL RUSSELL

WHILE WILT CHAMBERLAIN is unquestionably the greatest scorer in the history of basketball, he's not the game's most valuable player. That honor goes hands down to Bill Russell, the man primarily responsible for transforming the Boston Celtics from perpetual bridesmaids to perennial champions. All of the Celtics' successes date from 1956, the year Russell joined them. In the seasons between then and 1962, they lost only one N.B.A. title, to St. Louis in 1958. Russell sprained his right ankle early in the playoffs that year, was below par all through the series and missed two of the final games altogether.

The huge Celtics center—he stands close to six feet, ten, and weighs 220 pounds—is in a class by himself as a defensive star. The greatest rebounder who ever lived, he can out-jump anyone in the game. Add to this his determination, his killer instinct, his fighting spirit and, perhaps above all his pride, and the result is an almost unbeatable combination. No matter how great others may be, sooner or later they have to face Russell, and, more often than not, he stops them in their tracks.

Russell outplayed Chamberlain in face-to-face action so consistently that the Warriors finally moved from Philadelphia to San Francisco so they could compete in the Western Division where they thought they'd have a better chance to win. The Celtics had won the Eastern title six years in a row by 1962, and there was no sign of a letup. Since Russell was only twenty-eight then, the chances of the Celtics slipping in the foreseeable future were not much better than they had been in the immediate past.

Never a hot shot or a big scorer in the pro league, Russell has no ambitions in that direction. "I'd rather be what I am with a champion," he says, "than be the best scorer in the world with a team that never wins."

While he didn't mean to cast any reflections on his close friend, Chamberlain, the picture he drew of his archrival was pretty obvious. Russell has tremendous respect for the Warriors' miracle man, but he doesn't envy him. He's quite satisfied to be Bill Russell.

As such, he has revolutionized the league. Russell, a colorful performer, put glamor into defensive play. His job is to hold down the opposition, and he does it with remarkable efficiency. No one is better at blocking shots from any angle and any height. No one is harder to fake out of position or to get around, through or over.

Russell was the first professional to play the ball instead of the man. Others watch their opponents; Russell never takes his eye off the ball. Others try to keep their opponents from shooting; Russell dares them to, then, with his marvelous spring, bats the ball away before it reaches the basket. He can't stop everything, but he stops enough to keep the game under control.

The Celtics are a great team, but every one of its men knows that, as a general rule, they go as Russell goes. If he has a bad night, they usually lose. If he has a good one, they win, or at least come very close. When he's in action, they're the toughest team in the league to beat. When he isn't, they're a solid basketball team, but beatable.

In 1962, Russell missed four games because of a muscle strain—and the Celtics lost all four. It was the first time in five years that they had that long a losing streak. It inspired a Boston writer to these lines of doggerel:

"The Celtics had hustle—but they didn't have Russell,
So naturally wound up—losing the tussle."

Russell finally returned, and loyal Celtics followers breathed a long, collective sigh of relief. It was well-timed. With Bill back in action, the club won six straight.

"I guess that proves what makes the Celtics click," said Jack Twyman of the Royals. "Without Russell, they can be had."

Before nearly every ball game, Russell looks as if he can be had. The big guy has a nervous stomach, and gets so deathly sick that sometimes it seems certain that he can't recover in time to get into the game.

More than once he has said to Red Auerbach, the Celtics' coach, "I'm dying, Red. I can't make it."

Auerbach, who knows his star like the back of his own hand, is always sympathetic. "You just take it easy, Bill," he says. "And don't worry. We'll start somebody else if you don't feel better by game time."

Russell's fluttering stomach hasn't kept him from answering an opening whistle yet.

Sometimes, the tension is so great that he gets just as sick after a game as before. The final game of the 1962 playoffs between the Celtics and the Los Angeles Lakers was one of the most pressure-packed ever played. With the score tied, Russell leaped up in the last second, and blocked a Frank Selvy shot that would have settled the ball game, then grabbed two key rebounds in the overtime period to help give the Celtics the title. With 40 rebounds and 30 points, Russell was the outstanding man on the floor.

When the game was over, he blindly followed his mates to the locker room, got deathly ill, then wept. Only after that did he regain enough composure so that he could talk coherently.

Fred Schaus, the Los Angeles coach, gave Russell the lion's share of the credit for the Celtics' victory. "And the trouble is," Schaus added, "there's still no one on the horizon who can counteract the things Russell can do to you. The Celtics will be strong until they lose him."

Mindful of what Russell means to his ball club, Walter Brown, the Celtics' owner, pays him close to $40,000 a year, and doesn't begrudge him a cent. Brown first signed Russell for $24,000 in 1956, and has been giving him well-deserved raises ever since. It doesn't bother Brown that Russell still isn't among the best shooters in the business.

"You can always get shooters," he once said. "Where can you get Russells?"

Bill was so sensitive about his poor shooting that he once said to Auerbach, "Red, I can't find the hole in the basket. Hadn't I better quit trying?"

"You'll never find it if you don't keep on shooting," the coach replied. "But don't let it bother you. You're not paid to score points."

Even when Russell first went to Boston, the Celtics

weren't looking for point men. This had never been a problem for them. Every year since 1951 they had led the league in scoring—and in almost every year they had been the team most heavily scored on. The result was that they won no titles, and didn't look as if they ever would.

Then Auerbach sent Ed Macauley and Cliff Hagan to St. Louis for the right to dicker with Russell. Although there were a few shaky months when there was doubt that Russell would go into the N.B.A. at all, the trade paid off handsomely when Bill finally signed.

He gave the Celtics—indeed, the entire league—a shot in the arm duplicated only when Chamberlain came into the league three years later. Russell's amazing defensive antics drew customers wherever the Celtics played. In cities like Philadelphia, New York, Fort Wayne and Minneapolis, where there had been no sellout crowds for years, the fans flocked to see Russell.

In a game where the big emphasis is on offense, Russell is the only man who can get people out to watch defensive play. This is the most apparent when he and Chamberlain meet head on. Chamberlain is the scoring marvel, but the fans seem to enjoy seeing Russell stop him as much as seeing Wilt stuff in points.

Their first meeting, on November 7, 1959, filled the Boston Garden. It was an historic battle, clearly won by Russell. Both men played the full 48 minutes. Chamberlain scored 30 points to Russell's 22, but this was hardly a victory for Wilt, for he normally averages 45 to 50 points a game. Russell, on the other hand, rarely hits for more than 22 points anyhow.

Russell had 35 rebounds to Chamberlain's 28. The Boston center had the hottest foul-shooting hand of his career, sinking eight in a row from the line. Chamberlain, on the other hand, missed half of his 12 free throws. The big payoff in any basketball game is the result. The Celtics won by a 115–106 score. In the years since, they have beaten the Warriors by a ratio of two games to one, with each contest a battle of the two N.B.A. titans.

When Russell first came into the league, he found it difficult to cope with the roughhouse tactics. As a college boy, he towered so far above most of his opponents that he could toy with them. As a pro, he was pushed and pulled and mauled and hauled all over the place. Just as in the case of Dolph Schayes, who had to be told by his coach to hit back when he was belted, Russell had to be told by Auerbach.

"All you have to do is pop one guy," Red told him. "Nobody will bother you after that."

But it took weeks for the friendly, easy going Russell to take the advice. Finally, Ray Felix, six-foot, eleven-inch Knickerbockers center, gave Bill one elbow in the ribs too many. Russell swung and knocked his huge tormentor cold. It cost him a twenty-five-dollar fine, but it was worth it. Only once or twice in the years since has an opponent tried to give him the works.

Bill, son of a foundry worker, was brought up in Oakland, California. He entered McClymonds High School under what he considered a handicap. His older brother, Chuck had been one of the best all-round schoolboy athletes in Oakland and Bill was expected to be just as good. But, while Bill was bigger than Chuck, he was very awkward. The sensitive youth, knowing that he couldn't outdo his brother, decided not to try.

One day George Powles, the basketball coach, stopped

him and said, "You're a big boy. Why don't you come out for basketball?"

"I couldn't make the team," Bill replied. "Those fellows are better than I am."

Powles looked him carefully up and down, then quietly said, "Son, if you think they're better—they are." Then he walked away.

It was a lesson Bill never forgot, for that was the seed that planted in him the pride that makes him a super-star.

He went out for basketball the next day, and played two years on the varsity. During this period he didn't make enough of an impression to get mention on any of the Bay Area's all-scholastic teams. But he was growing fast, and had occasional good games. An assistant coach at the University of San Francisco saw him play one of them and offered Bill a scholarship.

"I lived right across the bay and didn't even know there was a University of San Francisco," Russell said later. "It was the only scolarship offer I got, and I took it."

It was a happy move for both Russell and the Dons. Until he came along, they had never won national prominence. But with the help of Coach Phil Woolpert and teammate K.C. Jones, Bill led San Francisco through two amazing seasons, during which the club lost only one game and won 55 straight.

The Dons were the hottest college team in America in 1955 and 1956. They won the N.C.A. title both years, with Russell twice hailed as the player-of-the-year and both he and Jones twice winning All-American honors.

Bill's biggest thrill didn't come on the basketball court, but in the White House. When President Eisenhower called together the nation's greatest athletes to launch his physical fitness program in 1955, Bill, who was a junior, represented college basketball. The President entered the room, looked around and said, "You all look bigger on television—all but Mr. Russell."

"Just imagine," Russell said later. "With all those wonderful athletes there, the President noticed *me*."

It would have been pretty hard for the President not to. Bill stood nearly half a foot taller than anyone else in the room.

Although basketball was always his sport, Bill went out for track because he wanted one of the button-down sweaters the university gave to the letter men. He was a great high jumper, who once tied Charlie Dumas at six feet, nine and a quarter inches in a state meet. Dumas later went on to become the world's first seven-foot high jumper. Russell also once broad-jumped 23 feet, seven inches, but gave up this event because he was afraid it would hurt his legs.

Bill graduated from U.S.F. in 1956, but refused to turn professional immediately because it was an Olympic year. He helped a team of Western college All-Stars defeat an East team, then sparked the United States team to an easy Olympic victory in Melbourne, Australia.

While the Celtics may not have been sure of him, Russell was never in doubt about his plans. The Globetrotters made him a huge offer, but Bill, who got married on his return from Australia, had no desire to clown his way about the world on basketball floors. He signed with the Celtics in December.

By that time, nobody was more used to the winning habit than he. Counting his last two years at San Francisco, the East-West college game and the eight triumphs by the

Olympic team on its road to the title, Russell had been involved in 64 straight victories. When he helped the Celtics to win in his first game with them, it gave him a string of 65, which must stand as something of a big-time record.

When the Celtics won their 1956 N.B.A. championship, it was Russell's third title within a year. San Francisco had won the N.C.A.A. crown just twelve months before, while the Olympic championship had come only six months after that.

In 1962, after the Celtics had won their fifth out of six titles, someone asked Russell how he could account for being on so many winning teams.

"I just don't like to lose," he replied quietly.

It doesn't look as if he will for a while either.

Wilt Chamberlain

20

WILT CHAMBERLAIN

A FTER ELGIN BAYLOR broke all N.B.A. scoring records with 71 points in a game against the Knickerbockers in November of 1960, he remarked, "This one won't last long. Chamberlain will get 100 one of these days."

It sounded like a cliché, since it seemed inconceivable for anyone to score 100 points in one game. But nothing seems beyond the reach of Wilt Chamberlain, and this magic figure wasn't either. On March 2, 1962, less than a year and a half after Baylor's prediction, Chamberlain scored his 100. The fact that the poor old Knickerbockers were again on the short end was not important. What counted was that Wilt, who holds almost every other record in the book, had pulled the most fantastic stunt in basketball history. A dozen years before, it had been unusual for a whole team to score 100 points.

But Chamberlain takes records in stride. He has been setting them ever since he came into the N.B.A. in 1959 as

171

the most publicized rookie of all time. After only three years in the league, he was catching up to the all-time scoring leaders of the N.B.A. By 1962 he had nearly 10,000 points, and was already among the top fifteen. Barring serious injury, he figures to be the highest scoring basketball player of all time by 1965, if not sooner.

In 1961 he became the first to score over 3000 points in a year; in 1962, the first to score over 4000. Since he improves with age and experience, the end is nowhere nearly in sight. This huge youth, who stands a shade over seven feet, one inch, is the most amazing basketball player the world has ever seen.

There have been others as tall, and one or two even taller. But Wilt, who weighs 250 pounds, is one of the strongest men in sports and one of basketball's fastest runners. He has terrific reflexes, a high jumper's leg spring and unusual balance for a man so large. Although no Baylor in the beauty of his movements, Wilt isn't awkward either. He knows how to get around without falling all over his feet.

Except for Bill Russell, the only man in the league who can consistently cope with Chamberlain, nobody knows how to stop him. Even Russell has reservations. Asked how he handles Chamberlain, the Boston star replied, "I use my own system. I try to keep him away from the ball and try to stay between him and the basket."

"What do you do if neither works?" an observer asked.

"Panic," said Russell.

Ed Macauley, who was coaching the Hawks when Chamberlain broke into the N.B.A., was standing in the Madison Square Garden lobby one night with Ned Irish, the Knickerbockers' owner, when a passer-by asked, "What defense can you use against Chamberlain?"

"Lock the dressing-room door before he comes out," Macauley said.

"And if that doesn't work, use an ax," Irish added.

After playing against Chamberlain for the first time, an N.B.A. backcourt man remarked, "You hear a guy is seven, one, and you nod. Then you face him on the basketball court and he looks like the Empire State Building."

A man of such stature is the natural butt of every trick, the target of every hostile fan and the guy most likely to get belted in a basketball game. Chamberlain has taken more abuse than anyone in the league's history, including even George Mikan, who absorbed a terrible beating in every game. But in three years, N.B.A. opponents never knocked Chamberlain out of a ball game, although they once nearly scared him out of the league.

That happened at the end of Wilt's rookie season, when the huge youngster came close to making a mistake that would have been remembered long after all his records were forgotten. He announced in a national magazine story that he was quitting because his opponents were picking on him and the officials were letting them get away with it.

It was the most blatant crybaby act since Little Lord Fauntleroy ran home to mamma, and the reaction on the part of press, public and players was a combination of rage and contempt. Chamberlain wisely changed his mind before the next season rolled around, and has since earned the respect of everyone who comes into contact with him.

Basketball players respect him for his adjustment to conditions which he found so intolerable at first, for his drawing power and for his sheer ability to score points. In 1962 he averaged more than 50 per game. His 100-point game in March didn't break Baylor's record, for Wilt himself had already done that twice. During the same year, he also broke about a dozen other league records, practically all of which were his own.

No man has ever dominated one department of a game as Chamberlain has dominated scoring in basketball. Because of his amazing ability to get under the basket and stuff the ball into it, he is the greatest drawing card the game has ever known. He fills arenas wherever he goes, even though he is no longer the novelty he was as a rookie.

But Chamberlain can hardly be called a great all-round player. He is not a clever ball-handler, and perhaps the worst foul shooter of all time. His average has been consistently below .600, and his playoff game average is less than .500. This means that he misses more fouls than he makes in playoff competition, and although he practices faithfully, he hasn't improved very much.

Chamberlain has always been a poor shot from the outside, for which the whole league thanks its lucky stars.

"If Chamberlain could shoot like Schayes," a veteran remarked, "nobody—not even Russell—could stop him. He would make a shambles of every ball game."

It is a source of great distress to this huge young man that he hasn't been more helpful to his team. The Warriors haven't won a division title since 1956, the last year they took the N.B.A. championship. The situation became so frustrating that they moved to San Francisco from Philadelphia at the end of the 1962 season, to get out from under the Boston Celtics.

"We couldn't win an Eastern Division title," one of their front office men said after the move was approved by the league. "Maybe we can win one in the West."

Inability to do any better on the coast will be Chamberlain's responsibility. This hardly bothers him, for, as happens to all big men and great stars, he absorbs as much blame for his failures as praise for his accomplishments. No one in the league takes more abuse for the Warriors' lack of success. There are fans and experts around the league who still feel that Wilt is not a good clutch player.

Yet no one depreciates his ability. "He gets the points, he gets the ball and he can go all night," Bob Cousy said not long ago. "What else can you say?"

"He's the greatest—just the greatest," Bill Russell, his nemesis and most ardent admirer, has said time and again.

"If he ever learns to hook with both hands, we can all go home," Elgin Baylor declared recently.

Chamberlain has been called everything from the Babe Ruth of basketball to the most fabulous figure in the history of sport. In some ways, he's a little of both. He's like Babe Ruth as a drawing card. He's fabulous in his remarkable combination of size, strength, grace and speed.

Wilt, born and brought up in Philadelphia, was a national celebrity at eighteen. By then he had attained almost his full growth, and was a living legend in Philadelphia schoolboy basketball circles. He was practically a one-man basketball team at Overbrook High School, and nobody found an effective way to stop him. Occasionally some team played four men on him, but this only succeeded in slowing him up, while permitting his teammates to shoot almost at will.

The rush among colleges to get him was ludicrous in its intensity. Over a hundred sent representatives to Philadelphia to sell their schools to this youthful giant. He made at least a dozen secret trips to campuses around the country, and listened to almost ten times as many offers. The fact that he was a good student made him all the more desirable.

When it became obvious that Wilt was not going to a college in the Philadelphia area, Eddie Gottlieb, owner of the Warriors, requested the N.B.A. to give him territorial draft rights to the youth. Even after these were granted, Gottlieb did a lot of waiting and sweating before he got Chamberlain's name on a contract.

The University of Kansas won the battle for the fantastic Philadelphia schoolboy, who already stood over seven feet when he entered college in 1955. Just why Chamberlain selected Kansas was never very clear. He later said the clinching factor was assurance by Negro friends that he would be treated well there. He was also a great admirer of the veteran Kansas coach, Phog Allen.

Allen was there only one more year, and Wilt didn't last much longer. He left school at the end of his junior year almost as mysteriously as he had entered. There were rumors, denied on both sides, that he couldn't get along with Dick Harp, who succeeded Allen as the Kansas coach. There were other stories that Chamberlain, a highly sensitive youth, didn't find life at Kansas as rosy as he expected it to be. Chamberlain always said that he couldn't afford to stay. The Globetrotters, who, unlike the N.B.A., are not restricted to signing college players only after their class has graduated, lured him off the campus with an offer of $65,000 to play with them for a year.

Despite the fact that Chamberlain did well in his classes as a foreign language major, it's probable that he got more out of the year with the Globetrotters than he would have by returning to Kansas. He played in the backcourt to build up his stamina and his speed. And he traveled all over the world, running madly up and down basketball floors from Tokyo to Timbuktu.

When the year was over, he was $65,000 richer, and a far better basketball player than he had ever been at college. And, to Gottlieb's everlasting relief, Chamberlain turned down all other offers in order to accept $30,000 to play for the Warriors. The Globetrotters would have paid him $100,000 to stay with them another year; an A.A.U. team offered him a $40,000 desk job for his basketball services.

He was, of course, an immediate success in the N.B.A. But from the very outset he was unhappy at the jostling he took in every game. In November of 1959, a few weeks after his rookie season began, Chamberlain said, "This is a rough game. I didn't expect as much shoving and holding and pushing. But I can't say I wasn't warned. They told me I'd be a target for everyone in the league, and I am."

He led the N.B.A. in scoring by over 400 points, averaging nearly 38 a game. And, although Wilt lost almost every hand-to-hand battle with Russell, he totaled nearly 200 more rebounds than the great Boston center. But after the Warriors finished second in their division and then lost the playoff semifinals to the Celtics in six games, Chamberlain made his sensational retirement announcement.

It was ill-timed and ill-advised, and brought the wrath of friends and foes alike down on Chamberlain's head. The youth spent the summer traveling with the Globetrotters, but even his friends in this group urged him to reconsider. In September he finally did, much to the relief of everyone concerned. He was back with the Warriors when the 1960 season began.

Although Wilt led the league in scoring and rebounds, and set more individual game records than the statisticians could keep track of, it was a bad year for the Warriors. They lost more games than they should have, and failed to

get by the first round of the playoffs. And, although Wilt
had adjusted himself to the beatings from foes, he wasn't
getting along with his friends. He disliked his coach, Neil
Johnston, and largely because of Wilt, the team was torn
by dissension.

Chamberlain was glad when the season ended, and
promptly left for Europe. The puzzled Warriors' brass, in
the meantime, knew it had to figure out some way to keep
him happy if the team was going to get anywhere. There
was every indication that it had not only the world's greatest scorer but one of its most temperamental athletes.

Gottlieb hired Frank McGuire, a highly successful
college coach and a man of great warmth, to succeed
Johnston, and the first thing McGuire did was make his
peace with Chamberlain. Nobody but the two knows exactly what happened, but they undoubtedly came to an
excellent understanding. When the season began, Wilt was
happier than he had ever been. And, although the team still
didn't win the title, Chamberlain not only had his best year,
but got along well with teammates and opponents alike.

Wilt is by nature a friendly man, but is sensitive about
his height. He travels far more than he has to, as if he is
looking for something that he hasn't yet been able to find.
A bachelor, he moves around at will, never staying in one
place more than a few days at a time.

He majored in foreign languages at college, and now has
good command of French, Spanish, Italian and German.
He loves sight-seeing and poking around in odd places, and
has been in most of the countries of Europe, including several behind the Iron Curtain.

Because of his stature, Chamberlain attracts attention
wherever he goes. He has been asked, "How's the weather

up there?" in a dozen languages. His standard answer is, "You think I'm tall? You should see my brother!"

His income, partly salary and partly from Wilt Chamberlain Enterprises, is well over $100,000 a year. He sinks most of his money in real estate, not only in his native Philadelphia, where he has purchased a $35,000 home for his parents, but in other parts of the country as well. He is in constant demand for appearances, exhibitions and endorsements and, with the help of a business manager, carefully selects those he considers most acceptable.

Now friendly, good-natured and no problem to anyone, Wilt has only one pet hate. He can't stand being referred to as "Wilt the Stilt." His friends call him "Dip" or "the Dipper," a nickname derived from the way he bends over before shooting. He likes that, and wishes the name would become as universal among fans as players.

"Dip," "Wilt the Stilt" or whatever, this young man is one of the truly great athletes the sport world has ever known. Now that his more serious problems have been unraveled, he's also a credit to his race and to basketball.

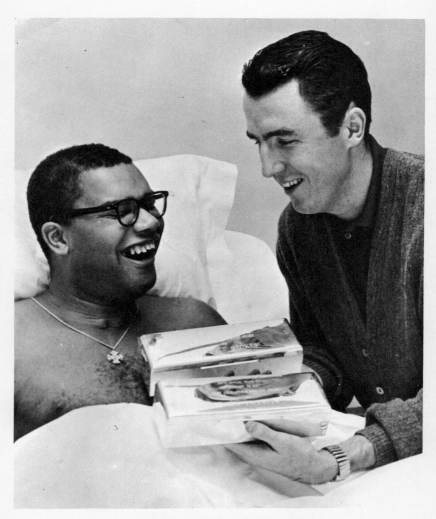

Maurice Stokes with Jack Twyman.

21

JACK TWYMAN AND

MAURICE STOKES

W ITH the help of a special sling, an almost totally paralyzed patient in a Cincinnati hospital room laboriously tapped the keys of an electric typewriter. The transcription of each letter was a major operation for the big man, since he was able to write only at a maddeningly slow pace. The typewriter was just beneath his fingers, but it took him long moments to move them from key to key. When he had finished at last, he called the nurse, and she pulled the paper from the machine. She read the message, turned away for an instant so he wouldn't see the moisture in her eyes, then turned back and said, "He'll like this."

The note read: Dear Jack—How can I ever thank you?

It was the only way Maurice Stokes, a Negro, could express his gratitude to his white friend, Jack Twyman, for devotion far beyond the call of duty or even friendship. The relationship between the two men serves as an inspiration

to everyone who knows their story—and it is one of the
finest ever told.

They were teammates on the Cincinnati Royals when
Stokes was stricken in March of 1958. His first sign of illness was nausea at the Detroit airport, where the Royals
were waiting for an airplane to take them back to Cincinnati. Stokes had to be helped aboard the plane, then became
alarmingly sick after it took off. While he was airborne,
his nausea became violent, his temperature soared to 106
and his breathing was so difficult that the hostess had to
give him oxygen to keep him alive.

Stokes was in a coma for four months. When he regained
his senses, he could neither move nor speak.

His ailment was first diagnosed as encephalitis—sleeping sickness—but the longer doctors studied his case, the
more doubtful they were. Finally, when Twyman remembered that Stokes had hit his head on the floor after a fall
at Minneapolis three days before the Detroit game, the real
cause of his trouble was found. Stokes was suffering from
a brain injury which had damaged his motor control center.

Meanwhile Twyman, the only member of the Royals who
lived in Cincinnati during the off-season, almost casually
took charge of the situation. Stokes's parents, his married
twin sister and his brother all went to Cincinnati when he
was hurt, but they couldn't stay indefinitely. His mother and
sister did what they could but neither was a professional
nurse, and Stokes had to have constant, expert attention.
The expenses facing the family were staggering.

A few days after arriving in Cincinnati, Maurice's discouraged mother asked desperately, "What are we going
to do?"

"Don't worry," Twyman said. "I'll take care of everything."

He was not indulging in heroics, for he was a sound businessman, as well as a good basketball player. Among other things, Twyman owned an insurance business at the age of twenty-six, and he was also a television sports commentator in Cincinnati. He had influential friends there, and he knew how to get them to help Stokes.

So, when he told Mrs. Stokes not to worry, he meant it literally. From that day on, Twyman has supervised all of Stokes's nonmedical affairs. He got himself appointed Stokes's guardian, then went about arranging for the payment of current and future expenses.

He knew that Stokes had a bank account, but he had to check nine Cincinnati banks before finding it. There was $9000 in Stokes's name, and Twyman arranged to draw on it when necessary. He got the National Basketball Association to designate a Cincinnati basketball doubleheader as a Stokes benefit, and it netted more than $10,000. Everyone, even the players, paid admission.

The publicity attracted more money. Kutsher's, a country club in the Catskill Mountains, ran an N.B.A. All-Star game which raised almost $6000, and the game has become an annual affair for Maurice Stokes. Contributions poured in to Twyman from many parts of the country. One man sent a substantial check, with a note reading: Where but in this country would I, a Jew, be sending money to you, a Catholic, to help a Negro?

When Stokes was first stricken, he was taken to St. Elizabeth's in Covington, Kentucky, the nearest hospital to the airport. The Royals paid all the bills while Stokes was there. When he could be moved, he was transferred to Christ Hospital in Cincinnati.

Then, after proving legally Stokes's ailment was the result of a basketball injury, Twyman got the state, through workmen's compensation, to take over Stokes's hospital expenses. That alone took the heaviest pressure off the shoulders of the family.

But Twyman didn't stop there. He visited Stokes three or four times a week, and often remained for hours. When Stokes still could neither move nor speak seven months after he was stricken, Twyman devised Stokes's only means of communication.

Stokes still had his mental faculties and he could still blink his eyes. When he wanted to say something, Twyman recited the alphabet, telling Stokes to blink when he came to the right letter. By repeating the process, Stokes could spell out words and sentences.

After a while, they devised short cuts, and soon Twyman could almost anticipate what Stokes wanted to say. Later he acted out charades, and that helped to speed things up. Soon Stokes's doctors, nurses and visitors were all carrying on conversations with him in the method Twyman had worked out.

During the summer of 1959, after Stokes had regained a little movement in his fingers, Twyman brought him a cardboard facsimile of a typewriter keyboard, and Stokes spelled out his wants by pointing to the letters. Less than a year later, Twyman acquired the electric typewriter which Stokes still uses.

As Stokes's therapy continued, Twyman worked with him under the supervision of nurses and therapists. When Stokes began to learn to speak, Twyman brought him a tape recorder. Stokes spoke into it, then listened to his own voice being played back, so that he would know what he was saying wrong and try to correct it.

With the help of a steel brace, Stokes now can walk a few steps between parallel bars, and he occasionally leaves

the hospital for short periods. He is even able to see the
Royals play basketball once in a while.

While Stokes will never again be normal, there is a good
chance that he might leave the hospital within the foreseeable future. He continues to take therapy daily, and he is
gradually learning to walk and talk. His finger movements
are increasing enough so that he might soon be able to get
more use out of his hands.

Actually, Stokes had to learn to do everything all over.
His paralysis was so complete that he was little more than
a vegetable for a long time. Everything had to be done for
him by others, and he couldn't be left alone for more than
a few minutes at a time.

As a basketball player, he was one of the greatest in the
business. Six feet, seven inches tall and weighing 250
pounds, Stokes won All-American recognition while putting
little St. Francis College in Pennsylvania on the sports map.
When he graduated in 1955, he was the Royals' first draft
choice, and he won the N.B.A. rookie-of-the-year award in
his first season. He was one of the league's outstanding
stars, and getting better, before he was hurt. He made the
All-Star team all three years that he played in the N.B.A.
He was the Royals' key man, the best rebounder in the
league except for Bill Russell of the Boston Celtics. Strong
and powerful, he made up in muscles what he lacked in
height. Even at six-seven, Stokes was not tall for a center
in the professional league.

Twyman graduated from the University of Cincinnati the
same year Stokes got out of St. Francis, and he was the
Royals' second choice in the 1955 player draft. Always a
great shooter, he improved after turning pro, and soon he
and Stokes gave the Royals a fine one-two punch. Stokes
got the ball off the backboard, passed it to Twyman and

Twyman's job was to sink the basket. Today, working with
Oscar Robertson in the job Stokes once had, Twyman is
still one of the best shots in the game.

Twyman and Stokes both grew up in Pittsburgh. Stokes,
born in 1933, went to Westinghouse High School, where he
made the All-Star public high school team in his senior
year. He and Twyman, who is a year younger, never played
high school basketball against each other, because Twyman
went to Central Catholic High, which played mostly paro-
chial school teams. However, they did meet in summer
basketball competition, but were only casual acquaintances.
Their relationship then was more a matter of mutual respect
than friendship.

They first became close friends at Rochester, where the
Royals were located when Twyman and Stokes each turned
pro. They suffered rookie pangs together and, since they
came from the same town and had mutual friends there,
they gravitated toward each other. As it happened, they
both loved progressive jazz and Broadway shows, which
they followed together.

Perhaps because there are only ten men on a squad and
all are in constant and intimate contact with each other
throughout the season, professional basketball is America's
most completely integrated sport. There are Negroes in
baseball and football, and integration among them is better
than it used to be, but it still doesn't compare with basketball. Negro and white basketball players have been rooming
together for years, just as Twyman and Stokes did from
time to time. This is the reason that the friendship between
the two went unnoticed before Stokes was hurt.

After Twyman was married, Stokes was a frequent dinner guest at his home. Carole Twyman, Jack's wife, considers Maurice her own friend as well as her husband's. She

visits the hospital as often as she can, making a special effort when the Royals are out of town. She has helped Stokes with his therapy, talked basketball with him and kept him company on a regular basis almost since he first got sick.

Twyman's admiration for Stokes is tremendous. "If it had been me," Twyman told a friend, "I'd have found some way to jump out that hospital window years ago. Maury just looks out and says he'll be out of there some day."

Twyman is one of the few outside the hospital who know what Stokes must go through in order to realize this ambition. Day after day, Stokes submits to five hours of therapy, some of which is agonizing. But he fights away the pain and insists on doing everything that must be done to get back on his feet.

As administrator of the Maurice Stokes Fund, Twyman guards the money as jealously as his own. The Fund is now fairly substantial. Thanks to Twyman, it has been carefully invested in gilt-edged securities. But there still isn't enough money. The day Stokes leaves the hospital, he will no longer draw workmen's compensation. From then on, he'll be on his own.

Contributions arrive from all over the country, from South America, and even from Europe. The association between the healthy white man and his ailing Negro friend has captured the imagination of people everywhere, sports fans and otherwise. This moves Twyman, but he doesn't enjoy it just for its own sake. The more people aware of the situation, the more money is likely to come in, and Twyman's most fervent hope is that there will eventually be enough to support Stokes for life after he leaves the hospital.

In March of 1960, Twyman won the Sportsmanship

Brotherhood Award for what he has done for Stokes. In accepting it, he said, "I want no recognition or thanks. I've gained more spiritually from the chance to do what had to be done than Maury has gained materially."

Since then, two magazine writers, Milton Gross and Al Silverman, have written stories about the relationship between the two men. Both gave their stories the same title, "His Brother's Keeper."

Nothing could be more appropriate.

INDEX

THE AUTHOR

AL HIRSHBERG has lived and worked in Massachusetts most of his life. He attended Brookline High School and Boston University and it was during his college years that he became a correspondent for the *Boston Post*. After graduation, he joined the sports staff of the newspaper and covered various sporting events. He was then assigned as a baseball writer to travel with the Boston Red Sox. He left the paper in 1952 to become a free-lance writer. Since that time Mr. Hirshberg's articles have appeared in many magazines including *Saturday Evening Post, Look, Reader's Digest* and *Sports Illustrated*. He has written two adult sport books, *Basketball Is My Life* (with Bob Cousy) and *Fear Strikes Out* (with Jim Piersall). In addition, he has written several baseball biographies for teen-agers. He, his wife and two children make their home in Brookline, Massachusetts.